Praise for
#MoneyChat THE BOOK

. . . .

"For years Dorethia Conner Kelly has been a valuable financial expert in the community helping numerous clients achieve financial success and overflow. Finally...she has made her expertise and knowledge available in print. Kudos for #MoneyChat THE BOOK. Now consumers have a user-friendly, practical and much needed guide with simple steps to get out of debt and become financially independent."

Glinda Bridgforth, author of
Girl, Get Your Money Straight!, Girl, Get Your Credit Straight!
and co- author of
Girl, Make Your Money Grow!

"If you are tired of people simply telling you to manage your money better, but not telling you how, this book is for you. Dorethia has provided realistic methods for getting out of debt and preparing for the financial life you want now!"

Ryan C. Mack, author of
*Living in the Village, Build Your Financial Future
and Strengthen Your Community*

"Searching for a great long-term investment? Look no further than Dorethia Conner Kelly's new book #MoneyChat. Spend a few hours curled up with this financial guide and you will reap dividends for years to come as you learn how to get out of debt, set yourself up on solid financial ground, and prudently invest your money for your future."

Manisha Thakor, co-author of
On My Own Two-Feet and Get Financially Naked

How People are Changing Their #MoneyChat!

Although I earned a great income, I was never really able to save money. After working with Dorethia, I was able to see where my money was going and create a realistic financial plan that I could follow.

S. Johnson, Administrative Assistant, Washington, D.C.

Working with Dorethia was very eye opening. As she helped us match our behaviors and spending habits with the numbers, we realized unexpected expenses were stopping us from reaching our goals. We developed a fund for for those irregular expenses are now better able to forecast throughout the year and add to savings.

The Cordaways, New Haven, Connectcut

Dorethia helped me understand the mindset of paying myself first and how it was transferrable across several goals. I began to set aside a percentage of my paycheck not only for emergency savings, but also when I needed to prepare for a large purchase. This allowed me to save and pay cash for a previously owned vehicle as opposed to financing a new vehicle.

L. Corbin, Healthcare Professional, Detroit, Michigan

#MoneyChat
The Book

HOW TO GET
OUT OF **DEBT**,
SUCCESSFULLY
M A N A G E
YOUR OWN **MONEY**
A N D   C R E A T E
FINANCIAL SECURITY

Dorethia Conner Kelly, MBA

⚹Felicity Media Group, LLC⚹

#MoneyChat The Book

Cover design: Ashley Fulgenti Designs
Cover photograph of author: Shawn Lee Photography
Interior design: Jera Publishing
Editor: Sonja Mack

Published in the United States
by Felicity Media Group, LLC.
Detroit, Michigan

ISBN 978-0-9863383-0-4

Library of Congress Control Number 2015900547

Dedication

· ·

For my children and grandchildren, my prayer is
that you always have financial success.
To my mother, I love you, that is all.
To my husband Will, it's primetime, who knew? Love you.

Acknowledgments

. . . .

Thank you to everyone who helped me along the way, held my hand, offered advice, provided their referrals, and resources time and time again. This is the short list, there are so many more, too many to list. Please know that I appreciate you all.

Thank you LaKeisha Mallett, Manyell Akinfe-Reed and Lori Mello for contributing your wealth of knowledge to #MoneyChat.

Thank you: Kim Brooks, Glinda Bridgforth, Ryan Mack, Manisha Thakor, Alisa T. Weinstein, Gail Perry-Mason, Gia Parker-Maxwell, B. Valaise Smith, Romeo Clayton, Tamekia Ashford, Karen Cordaway, Shareeke Edmead-Nesi

Thank you Karen Cordaway, Elizabeth Durden, Robin Wooten and Lamont Corbin for sharing your #MoneyChat stories. You guys ROCK!

Contents

#MoneyChat: Changing What You SAY and DO With Your Money!

WATCH YOUR MOUTH! HOW MANY of us heard that as kids? Both of my hands are raised, my mouth was always getting me in trouble. You need to tell yourself the same thing when you hear yourself saying negative comments about your money! I have always believed that our words have power, if you are constantly saying the negative, you won't be able to achieve the positive.

I can remember, as a young woman in my early 20s, never really hearing anyone say anything positive when it came to money. Someone was always moaning about not having it, needing to borrow it or loaning it out but never getting it back. They couldn't pay bills, bill collectors were always calling—they just stayed stressed out about debt and never having enough money.

That's part of my own story. I've heard many others, including some about those who have more than enough money. So much that they were able to have whatever they wanted. They never heard the word NO, so there were no boundaries. People like this may not have ever learned how to live without an abundance of money until they were on their own, which was probably a major shock. Saying no to yourself and to others is important to changing your money habits. We each have our own unique situations, whether it's never having enough or not understanding financial boundaries, that influence what we SAY about money as well as what we DO with it.

That's exactly what the #MoneyChat movement is about—changing what you say about money so your actions will follow! In my financial coaching practice, there are three recurring things people want to do:

1. Get out of the debt hole

2. Learn how to manage their money

3. Grow their money by investing and saving for retirement.

Many just don't know how to make that happen, so I wanted to write a book that spoke to those concerns. I also added chapters about IRS debt and gambling, because these are important money issues that are crippling millions of families, but they're not discussed as much mainstream.

At the foundation of changing your financial future, is building an emergency fund. In this chapter I share my experience and how you can start an emergency fund, bit by bit—even when money is tight.

Throughout each chapter in this book, I've included an action for you to take. It makes no sense to simply read what to do and not have some accountability. In my financial and business coaching practice I always give homework, so each chapter gives you 'homework' as well. Please share your success stories with me at dorethia@themoneychat.com and connect with us below.

 Join our Facebook Community

 Follow #MoneyChat on Twitter

Thank you for reading!
Here's to changing *YOUR* #MoneyChat!

Getting Out of the Hole

CHAPTER 1

Don't Manage Your Debt—Get Rid of It!

#MoneyChat

"Rather go to bed without dinner than to rise in debt."

BENJAMIN FRANKLIN

HEAR A LOT ABOUT DEBT management and it makes me cringe. It just seems that if you are only trying to "manage" your debt, you will always have debt. So, there needs to be a disclaimer. Yes, you need to manage your debt *but* with the end goal of getting rid of it. Managing debt means paying creditors on time, watching your credit score and not incurring any new debt. Getting rid of debt includes all of these, plus making extra payments to pay it down faster and, ultimately, eliminate it. That is the only way to get out of the hole.

Getting out of debt takes discipline. I know, we've all heard that before, right? Some joke about it: *I'll never get out of debt, I like having a new car every three years, I love to shop too much, it's the only way I can go on vacation*—you fill in the blank. All these excuses stem from not wanting to make the sacrifice and do the work required to live life differently, to save for the "fun" stuff as opposed to borrowing for it.

It takes action, sacrifice and hard work, but the payoff is peace of mind along with more money to spend, save and invest. Got it? Good! Now, let's get into the nitty-gritty!

Get Organized

Who do you owe?

Find those old notices, pull out those shoeboxes, look in those junk drawers. It's time to face the music.

List the debts you know of and get a copy of your credit report to see what may be outstanding that you've forgotten about.

List all your debts—even the ones you aren't currently paying.

- **Creditor**
  Who do you owe?
- **Purpose**
  Why do you have this debt? What did you use it for?
- **Interest rate**
  How much does it cost you to borrow?
- **Balance**
  If you were to pay the debt off today, how much would you need?
- **Monthly payment**
  How much is due each month?
- **Due date**
  What day is the monthly payment due?

You can track this information in a list like the one below.

Creditor	Purpose	Balance/ Payoff Amount	Interest Rate	Monthly Payment	Due Date
Capital One Credit Card	Build Credit	$8,601	21%	$150	15th
GMAC	Car Payment	$7,232	15%	$346	1st
Art Van Furniture Store	Living Room	$1,500	15%	$175	30th

What I like about writing it out like this, especially listing the purpose, is that it allows you to face yourself and your habits with debt head on. In the example above, it says the purpose of the Capital One Credit Card was to build credit. The strategy is to get a credit card, make a purchase and pay it off each month. It is really a strategy for people who are financially stable, but want to up their credit score. As you can see, this cardholder did not follow through as planned and ended up in a lot of debt. Defeating the purpose right? RIGHT! Hopefully never again.

Negotiating With Creditors

You want to deal directly with creditors so try to make arrangements with them before they send your debt to a collection agency that will add on their fee for you to pay as well. Once you and the creditor have agreed on a monthly payment or a payoff arrangement, get that agreement in writing before you send your payment. Also, do not give creditors your bank account information or allow them to automatically withdraw from your account. I got burned once because I gave a creditor my bank account information. Instead of taking the agreed upon amount, they took the entire balance due! When I cried foul, the rude account representative replied, "So what? Sue us!" From then on, I mailed or sent electronic payments via online banking.

If your payments have been late or you haven't been paying at all, you may not be able to negotiate a lower interest rate or payment. But if you have a lump sum of money, you will most likely be able to strike a deal. Creditors would rather get some of their money than none at all.

Credit Cards

If you are in good standing with your credit cards, you can negotiate a lower rate by checking the rate others received at: https://www.savvymoney.com/reduce-rates. Simply find the lender on the site, put in your balance and the site will tell you the average interest rate others received. The site also provides talking points and tips for negotiating with that lender.

Pay It Off!

Once you've made your list and have completed your negotiations, it's time to start paying your debt off. I'm a fan of the Debt Snowball Method of debt elimination because I know it works. With this method, you pay your debts from the smallest to the largest, in that order, regardless of interest rate. Why the smallest debt first? Well, because you gain some traction and a sense of accomplishment as you pay off each one. It feels better to knock off three debts at $250 each than to start chipping away at $10,000 right off the bat.

I've used the Debt Snowball Method to pay off a significant amount of debt myself. Over the years, I've shown my clients this simple process and those who use it have paid off a ton of debt. I don't believe in reinventing the wheel. I just find what works and do it. Simple as that!

How the Debt Snowball Method works:

Pay Down Your Debt, Smallest to Largest

	A. Dentist Bill		B. Credit Card		C. Car Payment	
	Amt Owed	Mthly Pmt	Amt Owed	Mthly Pmt	Amt Owed	Mthly Pmt
Month 1	280	50	1,700	100	12,000	350
Month 2	230	50	1,600	100	11,650	350
Month 3	180	50	1,500	100	11,300	350
Month 4	130	50	1,400	100	10,950	350
Month 5	80	50	1,300	100	10,600	350
Month 6 - Paid Off A. Dentist Bill	30	30	1,200	100	10,250	350
Month 7			1,100	150	9,900	350
Month 8	*Now use $50 from A to help pay off B faster.*		950	150	9,550	350
Month 9			800	150	9,200	350
Month 10			650	150	8,850	350
Month 11			500	150	8,500	350
Month 12			350	150	8,150	350
Month 13			200	150	7,800	350
Month 14 - Paid Off B. Credit Card!			50	50	7,450	350
Month 15					7,100	500
Month 16		*Now use $150 from B to help pay off C faster and so on until you are debt free.*			6,600	500
Month 17					6,100	500
Month 18					5,600	500
Month 19					5,100	500
Month 20					4,600	500
					4,100	500

*Note: When listing your debts, do not include your mortgage.

The mortgage isn't included because it is generally one of your largest debts. In certain cases I also suggest clients place student loans in the same bucket as mortgages. In those instances you continue to make monthly payments, but tackle their payoff once your other debts have been taken care of. Again, each case is different, there is no cookie cutter solution, this is just a general rule I follow.

Should I Consolidate My Debt or Use a Credit or Debt Counseling Agency?

Though I don't openly promote these services, I'm not totally against debt consolidation or debt counseling companies, because I realize that everyone is not a do-it-yourselfer. However, I do caution people to read the fine print and make sure they're clear on the services being offered and the fees being charged as there are many scams. It's important for you to know that no one can erase your debt or wipe your credit report clean, I don't care how much money you give them. Don't fall for it!

Debt Consolidation

When you consolidate your debts, you are taking out a new loan with a lower interest rate and monthly payment in order to roll several loans into one. Though the new loan will be the same amount, it may extend the life of the individual loans that comprise it because it's considered "new" debt. There are fees associated with debt consolidation but there shouldn't be an "up front" fee. So please read the fine print.

Credit/Debt Counseling Agencies

A good debt counseling agency not only negotiates with your creditors, it provides education and solutions to help improve how clients manage money in the future. There may be a startup fee but it should be under $50. Your monthly fee may be around $20. The debtor (you) sends one lump sum payment to the counseling agency, which then pays the creditors on the debtor's behalf. Here's the tricky part. Many people send their money to agencies that aren't reputable and the creditors never receive any payments. Now the creditors are adding late fees to the debtor's account and sending collection notices, all while the debtor is unaware and out of the money.

How do you find a reputable credit/debt counseling agency?

1. Look for at least three companies that have been around for a while—anywhere from five to 10 years. They will have online reviews from customers that you can use in your decision making. There are websites that will show you a comparison and rating of various agencies.

2. Compare the fees and services each company offers. What will they deliver for you? There are also sites that will show you a comparison of company services.

3. Visit the following websites to find an accredited company:

   a. National Foundation for Credit Counseling (NFCC); www.nfcc.org

   b. The Association of Independent Consumer Credit Counseling Agencies (AICCCA); www.aiccca.org

Robin's Journey to Getting Out of Debt

When I began working with Dorethia, I was at a point in my life when I knew it was time to make a change in my family's finances. I was one of those people who always looked the part; you would never know my husband and I were living from paycheck to paycheck. We earned decent incomes, but spent it all and then some, relying totally on our next paydays. That was normal for us; we didn't see the need to save. People looked at me and thought I had it all together. In reality I was wearing a sharp pair of shoes that I hadn't even paid for yet.

I was very excited to work with Dorethia. I took her suggestions very seriously, except when she said I should do my own hair for a few months. I was used to getting my hair done several times a month. That was a hard pill to swallow, but I eventually came around. I saved over $140 per month to add to our debt payoff. (My weekly visits were $75 each; I cut them down to twice a month.) We began tracking our income and expenses, stopped using credit cards, and ate at home more. We discontinued our cable service, a $125 per month savings, and used that money to build our emergency fund. That was the first step in our coaching process: to create an emergency savings, something we never had. We began to see results and finally had money at the end of each pay period. No more paycheck to paycheck living. It was a huge relief!

By applying what we learned in our coaching sessions and financial workshops, and by reading financial books, we were able to pay off two credit cards and pay down our other three cards. We stopped leasing vehicles and saved for a down payment on an affordable used car. Thanks to an improved credit score and low interest rate, we were able to buy a new home by putting 20 percent down in cash. Instead of buying new furniture for our home on 'time' or on credit cards, we paid cash. It took us about a year and a half to get there, but oh, it felt good!

We are so excited about this new stage in our lives. We've wanted to be debt free for a very long time. Now, it's a real goal we know we can accomplish.

CHAPTER 2

Gambling On Your Future

#MoneyChat

"At the age of 61, I lost my job, home, life savings, my retirement and my freedom. The worst thing was for my grandkids to watch me being handcuffed and put into a police car."

MARILYN L.

A GAMBLING ADDICTION DOES NOT FAVOR any one demographic. It affects all races, ages and income levels, and many have lost their life savings, families and careers because of it. Already a $120 billion-dollar industry in the United States, gambling is increasing with the onslaught of Internet gaming sites, new casinos and everything in between. Often thought of as a recreational pastime, gambling becomes more than just fun for many who find themselves unable to control the urge to do it.

According to the National Council on Problem Gambling, an average of four to six million Americans are problem gamblers. Now I'm not talking about professional poker players who have honed their craft and compete against other players rather than the casino, which always wins. I'm referring to amateur poker players and casino gamblers who have become obsessed with winning and are spending their household incomes in an attempt to hit the jackpot.

Compulsive gambling is an addiction that can afflict anyone. Often, people who have overcome another addiction—smoking, drugs, alcohol—turn that same compulsive behavior toward something else, like gambling. It can turn into a vicious cycle if the behavior is not checked and an opportunity to play a game of chance—in any form—can easily get out of hand. The frequency of the habit can quickly accelerate and lead to maxed out credit cards, defaulted loans and pawned valuables, all in an effort to get more money to gamble with. This explains why many compulsive gamblers end up filing bankruptcy. And that's just the financial damage a gambling addiction can cause. Compulsive gambling can lead to loss of employment and ruin family relationships, too.

Let's look at Marilyn L. who was never a gambler and who was 53 before she ever walked into a casino. She was hanging out with a friend at a weekend bowling tournament and they decided to try their luck. Marilyn sat down at a slot machine and won every time she played. She couldn't believe it! She decided that this was the way to go, that she wasn't going to have to work much longer because gambling was going to make her rich!

Marilyn and her boyfriend began making the four-hour trip from her home in Yuma, Arizona, to a casino in Laughlin, Nevada every weekend but, of course, her winning streak didn't last. Soon she needed more money than her paycheck could provide. Marilyn worked as an office administrator and, though she didn't handle cash, she had access to checks. She began making checks out to herself to cover her gambling habit.

Seven years and $300,000 later, Marilyn was finally caught and sent to prison at the age of 61. The police handcuffed her at home in front of her family and grandchildren. She put it best: "I lost my job, home, life savings, my retirement and my freedom."

Then there's Bernard, who admits to using gambling as a way to escape life's issues. His choice? Lottery ticket scratch-offs. Seems harmless right? Not if you're buying them several nights a week, spending $150 – $200 a pop like he was. Initially, Bernard would only buy them occasionally as a diversion, during stressful times. Eventually, he needed to escape more and more often, until he was spending most of his income gambling. Since Bernard handled the family finances, his wife didn't know that her paycheck was paying all the bills while his supported his gambling habit. She would ask where all the money was going, but Bernard would blame it on the gas the car needed for his hour and a half commute to work each day.

I Can Afford to Gamble

It's important to recognize the difference between recreational and compulsive behavior. Recreational gamblers are able to set aside a certain amount of money, play with it and be done. But if you feel the need to keep going back, like you *must* win and will risk everything you have to do so—that's compulsive behavior and you definitely can't afford it.

Having money to gamble for fun could be part of your budget, i.e., setting aside a specific amount for recreation. But you would do that *after* your primary financial duties:

- Paying bills
- Saving
- Investing
- Giving

The balance left over after each payday is what you have fun with. Risking any of the above to gamble is a clear sign of a problem.

Here's another forewarning: Is the money that you're gambling with *all* of the recreational money you have? Using all of your "fun" money to gamble is another sign that there's a problem.

Help! My Mate is Gambling Our Money Away!

You stop at the gas station to put gas in the car and your debit or credit card doesn't work. Hmm, the system must be down. So you go inside and have the clerk swipe it for you. Sorry, ma'am/sir, but your card has been declined. Declined? You paid the bill. You know there's money in the account. But what you didn't know is that your mate has taken what's left of the money for the household expenses down to the casino. Because they just know they'll hit the jackpot this time.

There are stories on top of stories about people who have depleted bank accounts without telling their mates. The money is just gone; there's no way to get it back. One woman sought help and stopped gambling for a while. She was doing fine and thought she could handle going into a casino—not for long, just for a moment. She figured she'd spend a little money and go home. At the time she was engaged to be married. Long story short, she gambled away her savings and her fiancé's in one sitting.

If your mate is a compulsive gambler, do not live in denial. It's important that you take immediate steps to secure the household finances.

Fact

According to the National Council on Problem Gambling, 20% of compulsive gamblers file bankruptcy.

1. **Get help.** Seek counseling for your mate's gambling addiction and for your marriage/relationship. Now is not the time to be passive—unless you don't value your financial future. It is important to confront your mate seriously and let them know they will lose everything if they don't get help.

2. **Remove access.** Don't allow your mate access to the bank accounts. Review all your bank and credit card statements to make sure you are aware of all activity. Request a copy of both your credit report and your mate's to see if there is any credit card or other financial account open that you don't know about. If you have joint accounts, it's definitely time to separate them until the addiction is overcome.

3. **Take control.** You will now have to manage all the household bills and other financial responsibilities if you didn't before. Prepare yourself, as this may cause serious arguments. You will have to be strong enough to stand your ground. If you do not, your finances will continue to crumble.

Begin to Rebuild Your Finances

Take a serious look at your spending/savings plan and stick to it. There are all kind of spreadsheets, apps and websites available to use. But don't delay, all you'll need initially is a pen, some paper, your bills and their due dates. See *chapter five* for the sample handwritten budget and recreate to fit your situation.

- If you are **in the black**, begin to pay extra on your smallest bill first. Refer to the Debt Snowball Method graphic in chapter 1.

- **In the red?** Well, it's time to start selling stuff and/or working extra jobs. Even if you're in the black, an extra job will accelerate debt payback.

- Stop using credit cards and make purchases with **cash only**. Cut up your credit cards. Close the accounts so you aren't tempted to use them.

- **Be patient.** You can lose it all overnight, but it will likely take you a few years to rebound. Keep notes; evaluate your progress every three months as well as each year. You'll be encouraged when you can see how far you've come, even in a short amount of time.

Action Steps: Keys to Rebounding Financially

The key to rebounding financially in any situation is to reverse the negative behavior or situation that caused the problems. There are resources for you, so make the call, visit the websites. Do whatever it takes to break free. Counseling is key when recovering from gambling or any other addiction.

- **Counseling:** Don't try to go it alone! You need the support of an understanding community. There's no need to be embarrassed or ashamed. Put that behind you and allow yourself to be transparent enough to win this battle! Schedule a counseling session immediately. If you can't afford to pay for counseling, there are many free support groups, such as Gamblers Anonymous. At the end of this chapter is a list of U.S. and international resources you can use or share with a friend.

- **Occupy your time:** Pick up a hobby, spend more time with your family—whom you've probably been neglecting due to the time you've spent gambling. Do not sit idly. Occupy your time with positive, uplifting activities so you're not tempted to gamble.

- **Stay away:** Block online casinos and gambling sites so you can't access them. In some states, you can have physical, brick-and-mortar casinos add your name to a list of people barred from entry. I definitely suggest this if it's available. Have an accountability partner who can monitor your whereabouts. Speaking of which ...

- **Accountability:** You need someone who will help you get on track with paying back your debts and managing your money. This may be the hardest part to handle, but until you've successfully completed your counseling sessions and are FULLY recovered, I'd suggest direct deposit for your paycheck and allowing someone you trust to manage your money, giving you cash for weekly expenses only, nothing extra.

An Expert's Take on Gambling Addiction

During this project I had the opportunity to interview Lori A. Mello, MA, LPC, MPA who is the Program Manager of the Michigan Problem Gambling Treatment Program with Health Management Systems of America. Our interview was so insightful that I decided to publish it in its entirety below.

What is the most common thread that you see in the gambling addiction cases you come across?

It seems as if no two cases are alike and yet there are very similar stories. We see people from all walks of life—the very wealthy, very poor and the middle class. If someone is addicted and wants to gamble, he/she will find the money. Some people say to me, "Oh, I don't have a problem with gambling. I can't afford to gamble!" I tell them that people will use their whole social security or welfare check, the grocery money, the rent money, etc. to gamble. It's really not about the money per se; it's about the thrill of the chase or the escape from problems at home or at work.

Many people have lost so much by the time they call us. Their home has gone into foreclosure, they've lost their car, their job, their relationships with their family, their spouse/significant other, children—they've burned bridges with everyone. Many have stolen, embezzled and are in danger of going to jail.

A lot of folks call the help line with a similar story. It might go something like this:

> *"I can't sleep. I go down to the casino (or play lottery tickets, or play Bingo) every day and I feel like I can't go without it. I have no food money for the rest of the month. I'm angry with myself. The bills are piling up. I'm scared because I'm three months behind on my mortgage and my wife/husband doesn't know. They repossessed my car. I lost my job because I spent three hours gambling at lunch instead of just one, and this was the fourth or fifth time I did that."*

Does recreational gambling lead to addiction or can it be something people do for fun, risk-free?

Most people who gamble recreationally do NOT turn out to be addicts. Addicts are only 2% - 3% of the population. Many, many people can be recreational gamblers and be just fine. What we always ask them is, "Can you do without going [to the casino] for a month?" or "Has gambling interfered with your relationships, your work, your schooling, etc.?" or "Are you losing sleep, not eating, not paying bills, going without things because of gambling?"

What are some of the negative financial results of gambling addiction that you have seen?

Oh, wow! What a great question! The list is endless. Here are a few things:

- Loss of home
- Loss of job
- Prison time for theft/embezzlement
- Putting oneself in danger due to the unscrupulous characters they might align with to get money to pay off debts
- Getting stuck paying restitution to one's theft "victims" or to the courts for many years
- Loss of relationship with spouse, significant other, kids, etc.
- Loss of transportation

What are the steps to overcoming a gambling addiction?

1. Recognize that you have a problem.

2. Ask for help.

3. Find the root of the problem. (Why are you gambling? What are you trying to avoid? What kind of thrill does it give you?)

4. Work on recovery through replacing the gambling activity with something constructive, something that gives you hope and satisfaction.

5. Don't give up! Attend Gamblers Anonymous meetings regularly to get ongoing support.

6. Find additional support outside of your therapist. (Who in the family or among your friends might be helpful or supportive?)

How have people bounced back financially once they've overcome their addiction?

It's very tough for them. Once you are behind like that, you have to work extra hard to fully regain your wealth and your retirement savings. You can't make it up to the kids if you can't put them through college. (Some people raid their kids' college funds.) Gamblers often go on a payment plan and take debt counseling, and that helps to get their debts paid in full so they can regain some good credit and be back on the road to recovery financially. Some are so bad off, however, that they need to file for bankruptcy. Others can simply do the debt counseling and repayment plan, which is much better than bankruptcy and doesn't ruin your credit for seven years.

It's a long and painful process. Gamblers also have to learn to live on less—to spend differently, to go without. They have to learn to do everything with cash and, if they have a spouse, to allow them to pay all the bills and give them an allowance. This can be very hard, especially for men. And especially for men who have been the primary breadwinners and bill payers.

For some of your clients whose lives are filled with opportunities to gamble—at family gatherings, online, in casinos, etc. What are some alternatives that have helped them break free?

This is where "harm reduction" really comes in. Gamblers have to decide what they want to do. Many clients will tell their family, "No. I cannot participate because that is an addiction for me. Once I get started, I won't be able to quit and I'm trying to stay in recovery." They may decide to just totally abstain [from the situation], even if the gambling is part of a family function. Sometimes, however, they do what we call harm reduction, where they limit their gambling money and/or the time that they gamble. They'll say, *I'll play for one hour and spend only $50.* Many people have supportive family and friends, so they can refuse and still feel okay.

If there was one message you wish you could drill into your clients to help them overcome a gambling addiction, what would it be?

That you will NEVER win against the house [in a casino]. The odds are set AGAINST you! There is no strategy to winning on any slot machine, in any card game, with Bingo, with the lottery, scratch-offs, Keno, etc. If you are doing this because you're unhappy with yourself or you don't want to face your wife/husband or your kids or your life, spend that money on therapy. Find out why you are unhappy and fill that hole in your life with something else before it's too late!

Can you recommend any national resources?

There are a few good ones, but most are state by state. The two that are the best to contact for more information are National Council on Problem Gambling (www. ncpgambling.org) and National Center for Responsible Gaming (www.ncrg.org).

RESOURCES!

GamBlock—Software that blocks access to Internet gambling sites. It helps people with gambling problems avoid the dangers of online gambling. Prices range from $35.00 to $70.00; www.gamblock.com.

Note: Parents, I'd definitely suggest installing this software on your teen's computers. There's an alarming number of teenagers gambling online without their parents' knowledge. Also, check their iPods, iPads and cell phones for games of chance.

National:

- Gamblers Anonymous (www.gamblersanonymous.org): an online international directory of meetings for those with gambling concerns and for the spouses, family and friends of gamblers

- U.S. National Gambling helpline (www.ncpgambling.org): 24-hour hotline, 1-800-522-4700

- Debtors Anonymous (www.debtorsanonymous.org), Phone: 781-453-2743, Fax: 781-453-2745

- Women Helping Women (www.femalegamblers.info): news and support for women in recovery

- Stop Predatory Gambling Foundation-U.S. (http://stoppredatorygambling.org/): resources to support the view that legalized gambling is harmful to individuals, communities and society

International:*

- Canadian Gambling Hotline: 1-888-391-1111

- Australia's Gamblers Anonymous (www.gamblersanonymous.org.au) provides information on GA meetings throughout Australia.

- GamCare-UK (www.gamcare.org) is a UK-based registered charity that provides counseling and advice through their helpline, face to face and through an online forum. GamCare-UK also provides education/awareness programs for young people.

- **Gamb-ling** (www.gamb-ling.com) provides multilingual information, awareness and prevention.

- **Gamtalk** (www.gamtalk.org) is an online support community for those with gambling issues.

- **Safe Harbor Compulsive Gambling Hub** (www.sfcghub.com) is a chat room and posting board for gamblers.

- **New Zealand Problem Gambling Helpline** (www.gamblingproblem.co.nz) is a free, national phone support service that also offers referrals, information and website support.

- **Problem Gambling Foundation of New Zealand** (www.pgfnz.org.nz) offers free counseling across New Zealand for problem gamblers, their families and others affected by problem gambling

* Source: www.problemgambling.ca

CHAPTER 3

It CAN Wait Until Payday!
Cash Advance Loans

#MoneyChat

I want to travel the country through underserved areas in a truck with an anti-payday loan message plastered all over it, shouting through a bull horn at the top of my lungs about the dangers of these types of money traps!

DORETHIA CONNER KELLY, MBA

What is a Payday or Cash Advance Loan?

A PAYDAY LOAN IS ESSENTIALLY MONEY borrowed to be repaid when you get your next paycheck. It sounds pretty simple, right? That is until you find out that these loans charge the highest interest rate of any loan option available, and that payday lenders are highly concentrated in lower income areas. Those two attributes make payday loans predatory and deceptive in nature. Many in these areas flock to payday loan establishments because they can't go to traditional banks to borrow when times get tight. It's understandable—the rent is due, the car breaks down, a sudden illness or other emergency pops up and cash is needed fast. Many of those who use these loans aren't financially savvy and may not understand that the interest rate they are going to pay is unreasonable. All they know is they need the money and this is the only place they can get it. It is easier than ever to get the money, but not so easy to pay it back.

It is well documented that these loans can end up costing borrowers between 400% and 800% in interest. Yes, you read that right. Enraged yet? Payday lenders dispute this, saying their loans aren't meant to be kept all year so they shouldn't be calculated that way. But the truth of the matter is that many people do end up paying on these loans for one or two years. This is because at least 50% of the people who borrow from payday lenders end up having to roll over, or extend, the loan.

How it works:

1. Borrower's bi-weekly take-home pay is $960
2. Borrower requests a $200 payday loan
3. Payday lender's fee is $30 ($15 per every $100) every 14 days = 15% interest
4. Borrower writes a check or authorizes payday lender to deduct $230 from their account (the amount borrowed + fee) on their next payday

The problem arises when the borrower still can't afford the $230 the next pay period and has to extend/roll over the loan. So you pay the interest on the loan—$30—and incur another 15% ($30 *more* dollars) because it's going to be another two weeks before you (might) pay back the loan. Now you're looking at paying 30% interest ($60) on a $200 loan.

How the 400% – 800% in annual interest is accrued:

1. $15 fee per $100 borrowed = 15% interest or .15
2. .15 x 365 days in a year = 54.75
3. 54.75/14 days = 3.91
4. 3.91 x 100 = 391%

It's easy to see how the interest you pay can increase to between 400% and 800% annually as you borrow more or keep extending the loan. This makes payday loans the worst solution ever for borrowing money.

A payday lender can look really attractive when you're in need. You could be facing a financial emergency that has you overwhelmed and you may not have the credit to go to a bank or credit union. You probably don't have a home to borrow against and asking friends or family—well, let's just say not this time. So a payday lender may be your last resort. I still say don't do it. They are predatory in nature and it is difficult to break the cycle.

Banks Are Getting In on the Game

Banks used to partner with payday loan establishments until it was prohibited by the federal government, due to controversy surrounding payday lenders. But over the past few years, several banks have decided to offer their own form of payday loan. They're called direct deposit advances or checking account advances and you can get up to $500. While bank fees (at $7.50 to $10.00 per every $100) are generally lower than traditional payday loan fees, they're still really high. The advantage banks have, however, is that customers trust them, see them as more reputable than payday lenders, and are more at ease borrowing from them.

How it works:

1. Bank customers are able to borrow up to $500 in any increment ($5, $20, $50, etc.).

2. The money is direct deposited into the customer's checking account.

3. In 14 days, on the next payday, the loan amount—plus fees—is withdrawn from the borrower's account.

4. If the money is not in the account, the account will be overdrawn and the customer will incur overdraft fees, as well.

While banks may not allow you to extend/roll over your loan like payday lenders, they do allow back-to-back borrowing. That is, customers can pay off one loan and immediately request another. But this can turn into the customer using these loans as a way of life instead of as the emergency fix the industry asserts they are meant for. Because the debt continues to grow and the interest continues to build up, the borrower is unable to stabilize his or her finances.

The truth of the matter is that most of the people who use payday-type loans can't afford to. They won't have the money to pay off the loans the next payday or the one after that or the one after that. Hence, the industry rakes in tons of money in fees. This explains why payday lenders continue to pop up in lower income areas, preying on the disadvantaged.

Action Steps: How to Avoid Payday and Direct Deposit Advance Loans

If you can take care of your financial emergency on the next payday, wait until the next payday. Payday loans are marketed all over the Internet and in underserved areas—even rich celebrities have begun to promote them! But they're really just a financial trap. Fortunately, many consumer advocate groups are fighting on behalf of uninformed consumers. As of this writing, 12 states have banned the operation of payday loan establishments.

1. **Reach out to your creditors.** Be honest about your situation and ask for an extension. In my professional opinion, it's better to pay the late fee from your creditor than to end up paying sky-high interest on a payday loan.

2. **Contact non-profit organizations.** Reach out to churches and other nonprofits that have emergency assistance programs. You will more than likely receive help with your financial emergency. The Salvation Army's and the United Way's 211 services are great resources.

3. **Ask for an advance from your employer.** Many employers will make confidential payday advances to their employees—interest free. The amount you are advanced is deducted from your next paycheck.

4. **Get a credit card cash advance.** Yes, I am anti-credit card, but I'd rather you get an advance from your credit card company

and pay it back immediately than pay 300% in interest on a payday loan.

Wait: Again, if you would be able to repay a payday-type loan on your next payday, then you may as well wait until then. There are also great income-increasing ideas in Chapter 6 – The Infamous Emergency Fund.

The Other Man –
A Payday Loan Horror Story

Michele was feeling financially trapped with no options. Although she and her husband both worked, their income was not always enough to cover everyday expenses and the extras that come with having three children. At the time, payday loan stores were popping up everywhere, and to Michele, they seemed like a way to alleviate some of the pain. She thought she could just repay the loan when she received her next paycheck. In passing, she mentioned it to her husband, who was adamantly against it.

Despite his objections, she decided to go ahead and get a payday loan, which began what she called her "affair with the other man," her secret payday loan sugar daddy. She couldn't see what the harm would be: All she had to do was prove she had a job, and with the next paycheck, pay the loan back, which she did. But, she couldn't stop going. It was like a revolving door that became an addiction whenever she found herself facing financial struggle. For two years, she secretly borrowed without telling her husband.

One day Michele sat down and tallied up the interest she was paying on the loans. That's when the epiphany came: she couldn't believe she had wasted hundreds of dollars in interest, money she needed to take care of her family. On top of that, she felt horrible about keeping this from her husband. She decided to stop her "affair" and get a better handle on her finances.

She began to prioritize spending and got her budget under control. She called creditors to make arrangements (and started honoring them – something she hadn't done in the past). Michele says she became transparent with creditors and told them what she could pay every month. She calls it growing up and not allowing fear and pride to take over. She faced her creditors, stopped letting her bills overtake her and began to see success in her finances.

CHAPTER 4

IRS - Uncle Sam is Not Playing With You!

#MoneyChat

"The IRS! They're like the Mafia. They can take anything they want!"

JERRY SEINFELD

NTEREST ON IRS DEBT IS *astronomical* and it compounds monthly. Don't listen to the ads that say they can wipe out your IRS debt. Though you can negotiate the penalties, the interest rule is regulated by law. There is nothing any IRS agent—let alone debt elimination company—can do about that. It's best to do whatever it takes to re-align your finances so that you do not owe in the future. In speaking to accountants, one mistake people make often is listening to others' tax situations and applying those solutions to their own circumstances. You don't really know the other person's entire story and could make things worse by not doing your own research and follow-up.

How People End Up Owing the IRS

1. Claiming too many exemptions on your W2, resulting in not having enough taxes taken out of your paycheck: Yeah, you claimed exempt for years and enjoyed all that extra money that belonged to Uncle Sam. You may fly under the radar for a while but the government's

payday is coming. And, trust me, it will be a big one! Okay, to be fair, some of you may not have known, initially, that you weren't having enough taxes deducted from your paychecks. I'll buy that for the first year, but year two, three and four? Uh ... NO!

2. Freelancers and small business owners: These two categories of taxpayer are responsible for their own taxes but often neglect to send in quarterly or annual payments.

3. Not filing: If you don't file, the IRS may file for you. You don't want that. The IRS will only give you the minimum deductions and credits—which works in their favor, not yours. They don't know how much student loan interest you paid, whether you made any charitable donations, how many exemptions you should be allowed, etc. Also, if the IRS files for you, you can't amend your tax return.

Make Arrangements to Pay

The IRS has a surprisingly detailed and clear explanation of their payment options on their website, complete with videos! Visit IRS. gov and click on Payments--but I've given you the quick and dirty version below.

Installment Agreement

When you find out you owe, call the IRS to request an installment agreement. This is most often the best option for those behind in payments. If you owe each year, you have to request a new agreement. You may be able to keep paying the same amount, but you need a new agreement, including the new amount outstanding. There are fees for setting this up. Learn more at IRS.gov when you click on Payments.

Offer in Compromise (OIC)

This is a settlement option where you ask to settle for less than you actually owe. You must apply to be accepted and meet strict guidelines.

From IRS.gov:

- **Lump Sum Cash**: *Submit an initial payment of 20% of the total offer amount with your application. Wait for written acceptance, then pay the remaining balance of the offer in five or fewer payments.*

- **Periodic Payment**: *Submit your initial payment with your application. Continue to pay the remaining balance in monthly installments while the IRS considers your offer. If accepted, continue to pay monthly until it is paid in full.*

Innocent Spouse Relief

If you file your taxes jointly and your spouse owes, you can file "innocent spouse." You'll have to prove you didn't know the taxes were underpaid.

Penalty Abatement

This becomes an option when, essentially, the IRS makes a mistake, such as giving incorrect advice or some other error. In this case, the amount you owe may be reduced.

Bankruptcy

This is a question I hear a lot: "Can I get rid of IRS debt by filing bankruptcy?" The answer is yes and no. There are a lot of rules and stipulations when it comes to being able to discharge your debt in bankruptcy.

The answer is NO if:

- You have current property taxes due within a year. Older property taxes may qualify as well.

- There are tax liens on your property.

- Your tax debt accrued as a result of incorrect tax refunds.

- You've had taxes collected by a third party.

- Tax penalties have accrued within three years prior to your filing for bankruptcy.

The answer is YES* if:

- Your tax return was due at least three years prior to your bankruptcy filing.
- You filed the return at least two years prior to your bankruptcy filing.
- Your taxes were assessed at least 240 days prior to your bankruptcy filing.
- Your debt is not due to tax fraud or tax evasion.

All requirements must be met and the debt may be only partially erased.

And what if you don't make arrangements to pay? Well, this is probably not the best move to make as the IRS has the upper hand. They can:

- Put a lien on your property.
- Garnish your paycheck, social security, retirement benefits or other income.
- Garnish federal and state tax refunds.
- Seize your car, home or other property.

Action Steps: Ensuring You Don't Owe!

1. Increase the withholding on your W4 and/or ...

2. Make additional estimated payments. Use an online calculator to determine the amount or do the math yourself.

    For example, if you owe, on average, $3,000 each year, divide that by 12 and that is the amount you need to send the IRS each month or have deducted from your paycheck.

$$\$3,000/12 = \$250$$

3. Current IRS debtors, do not ignore the amounts you owe. Call the IRS immediately and make arrangements to pay. You can also e-file payment arrangement forms when you e-file your taxes.

I haven't filed taxes in the last two years. I'm scared to file now because I know there will be interest and penalties.

Yes, there will be interest and penalties, but it is better to file this year than fall further behind. If you do owe, go ahead and call the IRS to set up an installment agreement with reasonable payments based on your income.

If you are owed a refund, you can collect up to three years worth. Anything past that is forfeited.

The IRS had Mr. Thomas by the Throat

Many people owe the IRS. Mr. Thomas owed every year, and paid according to his installment agreement. However, he added to that debt each year to the tune of about $20,000 in total. Now, I've seen people with much more IRS debt than that, but $20,000 is still a ton considering what the IRS charges in interest. Mr. Thomas earned about $40,000 more than his base salary by working overtime, but he never adjusted his exemptions or paid additional money each pay to cover the shortfall in the taxes withheld.

The first thing I suggested he do was fire his accountant, which was his wife. Thank goodness she did not get offended. Many people know how to handle the simple things in order to do their own taxes; she did both of their taxes using online software. No big deal, but when someone owes every year, you need an experienced tax professional to look at your tax return and show you how to adjust.

As I stated, the interest on IRS debt is outrageous. To continue to add to the debt amount each year is nuts, especially when you can do something about it. But guess what? Mr. Thomas did not want to adjust. Yep. He would rather owe and pay a ton of interest than miss that money in his paychecks.

Therefore, the second thing we worked on was a mindset shift. I showed him the math and how long-term vs. short-term thinking positively affects your finances. With his IRS debt, he would never get out of the hole if he didn't stop the madness and make sure enough was deducted from his paychecks for taxes going forward. He had to go home and think about it, but at the next session, I convinced him to make the change.

Next, I worked with him on a plan to pay off the debt over a two-year period. We explored making extra payments, cutting back on spending (of course), utilizing future overtime earnings, and selling investments.

At the end of the day, he was relieved to have someone hold his hand through the process and tell him what he needed to hear.

Getting on Solid Ground

CHAPTER 5

Get Your Money Right!

#MoneyChat

"You don't have to be a miser, just be wiser with your money."

DORETHIA CONNER KELLY, MBA

IN ORDER TO MAKE YOUR money grow, you have to manage it properly. It's important to get beyond having just enough or barely making it so you can focus on the larger financial picture--creating a nest egg for the next generation in your family.

Step 1. MAKE A DECISION

Making a decision to better manage your money is the first step to getting on solid financial ground. When you get tired of riding the same merry-go–round—never having enough money, hiding from creditors, facing financial emergencies—it will definitely be decision time! Now, this doesn't mean you'll get it right every time, but you will keep going in the right direction, learning along the way and never giving up. Eventually, you'll find that you make fewer financial mistakes and there's money in the bank!

It's not that easy? Okay, here's a little exercise. Get a sticky note and write down everything you'd be able to do if you only had to pay for necessities—that is, if you didn't have to make any debt payments.

Now write down how that makes you feel. Relieved? Like a burden is lifted? Happy? Stick that note up in various places throughout your home to remind you of your aim. Use it to light a fire in you toward making the decision to take action!

Step 2. GET BUSY! Be Your Own Financial Coach!

1. Educate yourself

What are you reading about money? Don't let Candy Crush take up all your time! Set aside time each week to read at least three articles about personal finances and money management. Everything won't apply, but the more you learn, the quicker you'll be able to determine what's good advice for you. Look up terms and words you're not familiar with.

2. Set financial goals

Write out your goals. What do you want to accomplish financially? Take small steps; don't think you have to write that you'll be debt free in three months if you know that isn't feasible. And don't only write down the goal, write how you will achieve it.

> **Example:**
> *This Year ...*
> 1. *I want to completely pay off one bill in six months by paying an extra $25 per month.*
> 2. *I want to save $50 per pay period, each month, by buying lunch only on Fridays.*
> *Three-year Financial Goals ...*
> *Five-year Financial Goals ...*
> *10-year Financial Goals ...*

3. Know your numbers!

Remember, managing money is really just simple math. What you have coming in vs. what's going out. As I said before, all you need is pen and paper and a list of your bills with their due dates.

Create four lists:

- **Income**—Amount of money you have coming in from all sources.

- **Expenses/Bills**—What bills and household expenses do you pay each month, quarter, etc.?

- **Current assets**—Any investments, savings or other valuables you may have, like that money in the safe under the floor boards (wink, wink).

- **Current debt**—For debts that you may or may not be paying monthly, what is the total balance due and monthly payment amount? If you were able to pay it off today, how much would it take to do so?

4. Develop a system

Do not freak out! This simply means having a schedule for paying bills/budgeting, paying off debt, saving/investing and reviewing your progress.

Here's an easy system to follow:

Budget:

- Budget bi-weekly or monthly

- Choose a "light," less busy day where you'll be able to focus quietly for an hour. For me, it's early Saturday morning before the house (my family) wakes up.

When writing out your budget, don't just consider the current month. Do three months at a time, at a minimum. This allows you to plan for the future months and re-adjust as needed.

Sample monthly budget:
Family of four, monthly net income of $4,200

		Jan		Feb		March	
		Budget	Actual	Budget	Actual	Budget	Actual
Income:			4,200.00	4,200.00		4,200.00	
Expenses:							
Tithes/Giving		-300.00	-300.00	-300.00		-300.00	
Savings:		-300.00	-300.00	-300.00		-300.00	
Housing:							
	Rent/Mortgage	-750.00	-750.00	-750.00		-750.00	
	Renters/Home Ins.	-100.00	-100.00	-100.00		-100.00	
Utilities:							
	Electric	-50.00	-44.00	-50.00		-50.00	
	Gas	-100.00	-125.00	-100.00		-100.00	
	Water	-35.00	-35.00	-35.00		-35.00	
Transportation:							
	Car Pmt	-325.00	-325.00	-325.00		-325.00	
	Car Ins.	-175.00	-175.00	-175.00		-175.00	
	Gas	-400.00	-375.00	-400.00		-400.00	
	Repairs						
Food:							
	Groceries	-450.00	-525.00	-450.00		-450.00	
	Eating Out	-100.00	-75.00	-100.00		-100.00	
Household:							
	Toiletries	-100.00	-55.00	-100.00		-100.00	
	Cleaning, etc.	-20.00		-20.00		-20.00	
Clothing:							
	Kids	-100.00	-125.00	-100.00		-100.00	
	Adults	-175.00	0.00	-175.00		-175.00	
Grooming:							
	Kids	-20.00	0.00	-20.00		-20.00	
	Adults	-100.00	-100.00	-100.00		-100.00	
School Expenses:							
	Kids	-50.00		-50.00		-50.00	
	Adults	-300.00		-300.00		-300.00	
Entertainment/Gifts:							
	Parties/Birthdays		-35.00				
	Movies/Concerts		-120.00				
	Holidays						
Total Expenses		-3950.00	-3564.00	-3950.00		-3950.00	
Balance (Income - Expenses)		250.00	636.00	250.00		250.00	

In this example, the month of January is over and the budgeted and actual
spending amounts have been entered. February and March are projected
spending amounts. As each item is paid during the month, you write in
the actual amount spent.

Budgeted vs. Actual:

In the example above the difference between budgeted and actual for January: $386

If you see that you're going over or under budget regularly, you need to adjust your spending. For example, if you budget $350 for groceries each month, but consistently spend $450, that is probably the amount you should budget for. If it's a stretch, see where else you can cut to fund it. If you find that you budget $250 each month for clothes, but only spend $175, lower your budgeted amount for clothes.

Eliminating Debt

Based on the numbers in your budget, is there anything left to add toward getting rid of debt faster? If yes, begin using most (if not all) of that surplus to pay off the smallest debt first.

Investing

If you are currently investing, determine whether you can contribute more each month. If you are tackling debt now, decide on a date— whether it's next year or in the next three years—that you'll be able to start investing.

I encourage investing after you've paid off as much debt as possible and only have larger amounts to bite off. Until then, all extra money should go toward getting rid of those smaller debts.

Quarterly Review

It's important to track how you're doing. Over the years, I noticed that it worked better for my clients to have a timeline for review that would serve as a reminder, so I suggest a quarterly schedule. As the seasons change, you know it's time for a checkup!

During your review, ask yourself honest questions. The point is to be making headway toward your goals. Are you consistently budgeting and sticking to it? If not, what needs to be adjusted? How much debt have you been able to pay off? Did you open that mutual fund account? Get that second job? If you had a setback or you aren't where you wanted to be, don't beat yourself up about it, just start over!

5. Accountability

Who do you know that is good with money? If you're married, think of a couple that's good with money. Who can you trust to discuss major financial decisions with?

I have a great group of friends. They reel me in when I'm in the deep end and encourage me when I need it. We need people like that when it comes to our finances. You should have one or two people in your circle that you can learn from when it comes to finances.

I know money is a personal and touchy subject--we don't want others to know how much we do or don't have, or how much we may not know about money. I understand and I'm not suggesting that you run to everyone you know and tell them your business. But think of a couple of people who are smart with their money. You can tell by their conversation and actions. I'm not talking about people who brag about what they have or look like they have it all together. No, find people who talk about things like saving and investing more than spending, people who talk about retirement accounts, getting out of debt and preparing their kids for college, and who are practicing what they preach.

A word about budgeting: I know there are a million schools of thought on this subject. Some say it's useless because people hate to do it and never will. Some try to do it mentally and end up miscalculating, forgetting about money spent, etc. I'm sorry, but writing out your budget is the first basic action you must take in successfully handling your money. It allows you to see how much money you will or won't have over several weeks/months so you can plan. It helps eliminate financial surprises from popping up.

I don't yell "YIPPEE!" every time I sit down to do my budget, but it's a necessary practice so I know where my money is going. And budgeting now is super easy with all the apps that are available and online banking. Once you put your info in once, you can simply adjust as needed.

I suggest you budget and pay bills bi-weekly or monthly. This allows you to better manage your time and it's not as much of a chore. Having to do it every week may be too much for some and cause them to stop altogether. So whether it's pen and paper, a spreadsheet or an app on your phone, get 'er done!

Lamont — Living the Single Life and Paying Myself First

As a single man with children, dating can be a challenge if not carefully planned out. Disposable income is hard to come by sometimes. While managing my bills (rent, utilities, etc.), I also want to have fun with the leftover funds from working so hard.

When discussing this with Dorethia, she emphasized a very important point that I took to heart. "One who saves early can afford big things for a longer time frame." Her suggestion was to "pay myself first," being prudent with my net income minus any bills I've already paid. The key is to set a target for savings just as if I owed myself a large bill that I had to pay in installments. Once I deducted that amount, she suggested a 'dating fund' for me. We laughed about it, the thought was hilarious to me, but I started doing it anyway. It worked, I set aside a certain amount I wanted to spend each pay on my single life activities. When the funds had been exhausted, that was it. No more dates or nights out with the guys. It worked and I was fine with it because I was able to get out and have fun while saving money for my future.

This saving mindset also helped with the purchase of my current vehicle. I had been looking to upgrade, but with my previous car paid off, I wasn't interested in financing a car note. Unfortunately, insurance can be expensive where I live as I reside in an urban area. As a matter of fact, insurance is so expensive that many times the cost exceeds what you would have paid for your monthly car premium.

Attempting to avoid this, I followed the same theme of paying myself first. The first step was deciding on how much I wanted to spend. I finally conceded to selecting a used car as the insurance typically wouldn't be as much. Because I live in a no-fault state, I could elect to lower my cost even more. I scoured many online sites and figured that a late model vehicle between $4,000 and $5,000 would suit me just fine. Knowing the time frame in which I wanted to purchase the car, I divided my biweekly pays into a reasonable amount and deposited into an account that was hard to access (to keep me honest). I did this by opening up an account with no debit card so if I needed funds, I would have to physically go to the credit union. To deposit money, I could just mail in a money order.

As I got into the habit of contributing to my "car bank," the process felt extremely fulfilling. Eventually, I hit my goal, selected a vehicle, had it inspected, and voila! I had the car I really wanted at an economical price. Plus, calculating that an average car note for a new car would have been at least $350 (once again, not including the *high* insurance in my area), paying for the car in full, in this case $4,200, meant that I essentially paid myself back in about twelve months, if not less.

In summary, I found that when I applied Dorethia's words of wisdom to pay myself first, the rewards I reaped were transferable across many goals. I really appreciate the advice she gave me.

The Durden Family

We are a blended family. My husband and I started dating around the time we found out how much money he was to pay in child support, which was and still is a lot. We dated for two years before getting married. I have two daughters, ages seven and four, and he has a daughter and a son, ages eight and three.

I have always loved learning about money and budgeting; it's fun to me. My husband's relationship with money was a different story. But, when we realized that we had to differentiate between what we needed and what we wanted, his eyes opened as well. I began following every money management website and expert on Facebook and Twitter, which is how I found Dorethia's #MoneyChat. I loved the guests and advice from participants; it showed me I was not alone on my path. My goal was to discover different perspectives on money management and what we could apply to our finances.

With all the information I was learning, we began to make life changes. My husband got rid of his new vehicle and got a fifteen-year-old car. My truck is twelve years old. We decided to live off one paycheck so we researched a low-cost area to live. Of course, as soon as you begin to get on a positive path, challenges come. In the first two years we were together, not only did we spend 40 percent of his check to support his children, but I also lost my job. Good thing we were living on one paycheck and saving money. Because we eliminated cable, car loans, eating out, and always looked for bargains, we were still able to eliminate all our debt in the same time frame. We paid off approximately $45,000 in debt ($25,000 was eliminated when he sold his truck). We were also able to take the *entire summer off* to spend with our children.

My husband and I were both in the military, which afforded us the opportunity to attend college without student loans; we both earned our bachelor degrees. My husband was still on active duty so the Army paid his tuition. Since I am a veteran, I used my GI Bill to pay for about 75 percent of my education costs. We paid the other 25 percent out of pocket.

When my husband was preparing to leave the military, he was required to take a budgeting class, which was a real eye opener for him. He always trusted that I knew why we were being frugal, but the class made him realize just how important it was. We complement each other in that he helps me see that sometimes we need to spend a little to create family memories and I make sure we don't spend too much.

We decided that our children need memories and experiences, not presents. We have fun every day and, most of the time, for free. We have picnics, go to playgrounds and on hikes, and share memories by making things from scratch. Now that we are debt free and have some money in savings for emergencies and other things, we are definitely feeling more relaxed and enjoying life more.

CHAPTER 6

The Infamous Emergency Fund

"Rocks in my path? I keep them all. With them I shall build my castle."

NEMO NOX

"THAT WILL BE $2,500, MA'AM."

"Whoa! What?"

"Yes. There's a lot of body damage. You'll need two new doors, front end work and paint."

My heart began to pound and suddenly my stomach didn't feel so good. I walked back to my beat-up truck, climbed in and cried that big, ugly, mouth wide open cry. As I was driving home from work that week, a kid slammed into my driver's side while pulling out of a gas station. I had worked hard to pay off my truck early and then, being even more ambitious, I dropped my insurance coverage down to basic—which meant this repair wasn't covered. (I'll never do that again!) I had no money in the bank and had never had $2,500 at any given time anyway. I had no idea how I was going to pay for the repair. I was already overextended and couldn't add anymore bills, and I refused to borrow any money.

I had been caught like this many, many times. Financial emergencies would come up and I'd have no way of covering them. As a single mother with two kids, there was never really any "extra money." One day, I was browsing through a website and saw an article about an emergency fund. *Now what is that?* I thought. As I began to read the article, I knew this was going to be the first step toward changing my financial future.

Emergency Fund: [ih-mur-juhn-see fuhnd]

A supply of money set aside for unexpected financial issues.

Game Changer:

From then on, I began to read as much as I could about handling my money differently, saving money and, yes, building an emergency fund. It worked! I was elated! But even more than that, I was relieved. It took some time, but I was able to actually save by changing my habits one by one.

Down the road, other financial emergencies arose--the refrigerator had to be replaced, there were more car repairs, unexpected medical bills, etc. But I was prepared. There was no need for tears or that feeling of dread and despair because I could write a check! Wooo Hooo! Not only that, but my conversation changed. I was telling my family and friends how they could avoid being broke all the time and succeed with their money. You can, too! Keep reading!

How Much Should You Save?

An emergency fund allows you to breathe easier when financial issues come up and, trust me, they will come up! How much you save depends on your comfort level, but the minimum, initially, should be $1,000. Young adults or those with extremely tight budgets may want to ease into it and start with $500, then build up to $1,000. And then savers and couples who can afford it may be able to save $2,500, initially.

There are two phases of saving for emergencies:

Phase 1: Saving for things that come up throughout the year. Once you've reached your goal, you can stop adding to the fund and re-allocate the money you were putting toward it to paying down debt. Be sure to maintain $1,000 in the fund at all times.

Phase 2: Saving nine to 12 months of expenses (not income) to cover major situations, such as a job loss or a medical emergency, *after* you've paid off all your debt. The debt I'm talking about here does *not* include your mortgage. That can be taken care of later, once your financial footing is more stable.

Now don't let saving nine to 12 months of expenses scare you. You'll still be able to live. Remember—you'll be working from your budget and all spending will be accounted for, even the fun spending! Set milestones. Save one month of expenses, three months, six months and so on until you reach your 12-month goal. Also remember—by now you will have paid down some debt, so you'll be able to save more money.

How to Save Your Emergency Fund

It's time to get creative, especially if your budget is stretched to its limits. If you're already in the red each month, you'll definitely have to focus on increasing your income to cover your normal household bills. Slow and steady wins the race. Pay the monthly amounts on your normal household bills, and any additional money brought in goes toward your emergency fund.

Think about every area you may be able to save. For instance, if your cable bill is $100 per month, you could save $1,000 if you went without cable for 10 months. After you've reached your goal, you can have your cable back. That may even be an incentive to save faster!

More month than money? Pay these first!

Housing – Pay your rent or mortgage first. You need a place to lay your head and you want to provide stability for your family

Utilities – Yeah, let's keep the lights and heat on. This is part of that stability mentioned above.

Groceries – When it comes time to cut, most people skimp on groceries. They buy junk with no nutritional value because it's cheaper. Well, I certainly hope you aren't at Whole Foods if you need to cut back, but it's important to feed your family healthy meals. Go to farmers markets and catch sales in order to save money.

Transportation – If you can't get to work, you won't have a job long, so make sure you have transportation, whatever form it may be in. Again, this doesn't mean you should run out and lease that new Cadillac Denali truck! Be sensible, just be sure you can get back and forth to work.

Ladies, hair and nails can really add up. I know—this is sacred ground and I truly understand. But add up how much you're spending on yourself and your daughters each month. A few months of sacrifice would get you closer to your goal.

Single fellas, the dating scene and hanging out with the guys can really put a cramp in your wallet and saving goals. I have a friend who said that, thanks to me, he's started a dating fund. That's right, an amount he can spend each month taking a young lady out to dinner, to a movie, etc. And when the fund is empty—no more dating for the month. Or maybe just some movie nights in.

What if you focused on your emergency fund for a few months and seriously cut your "hanging out" money? Sounds like a plan to me! It's not forever, just until you reach your goal.

Dig deep. Sometimes we can find money in places we never thought of looking. For instance, do you have investments, bonds, etc. that you can liquidate? Do you have valuables you can sell? Sites like Ebay, Amazon and Craig's List have made it easier than ever to sell things we aren't using anymore. Take inventory of your home, garage, basement etc. to see what you can get rid of to bring in extra money.

Okay, Dorethia. I've got nothing. There's no extra money anywhere! Well then, it's time to increase your income. It's time to look for another job in addition to your main gig and let go of all pride. That's right—it doesn't matter what the job is, as long as it pays. I've coached clients who earn well into the six figures, yet have no savings and live paycheck to paycheck. I tell them the same thing. Find a part-time job—or two!

Think of five things you can do for extra money, with the least amount of cash outlay. If you need ideas, check out the list at the end of this chapter. Here are a few to start with:

- **Home Cleaning** – All you need is a mop, a bucket, some cleaning supplies and you're in business pretty quickly!

- **Handyman** – Painting, garage cleaning, minor home repairs— these are especially helpful to seniors and single parents.

- **Auto Repair** – Brakes, oil changes, tune-ups—small jobs you can do from home.

- **Ebay/Amazon/Craig's List** – It's easy to sell items online. I have a friend who finds cheap books at library sales, yard sales, etc. and re-sells them online.

- **Take a Class** – Community colleges often offer classes in areas that you could turn into a profitable side business, e.g., landscaping, crafts, hair braiding, graphic design, minor auto repair, etc.

Where to Stash Your Savings

Your emergency fund is not to be considered an investment, so you wouldn't save it in a mutual fund, buy stock with it or otherwise invest it. This is cash that you need to be able to access right away if necessary. Therefore, it should be kept in a high-yield money market savings account, which has a higher interest rate than a traditional savings account. In the beginning, when you are building up to your $1,000, you may have to begin with a traditional savings account, then switch to a high-yield account once your balance has reached the minimum required. While the money is sitting and waiting for the inevitable financial situation or emergency to come up, it may as well collect as much interest as possible.

That's NOT an Emergency

Okay, let's get a few things straight. An emergency fund is not simply extra money. It has a goal, which is to keep you financially stable when the storms are raging. This means there's no room for any "I deserve it" or "pity party" purchases. This is about reaching your financial goals. If you use the money in your emergency fund to go shopping every time you're upset, feeling low or get distracted by some new car, tool or tech item that depreciates in value, you will be out of luck when an actual emergency occurs. So hands off! You want it to be there when you need it.

You know what else is NOT an emergency? Family members who are low on cash. If you have a tendency to go into your pocket when family comes calling, set up a separate fund for that. Seriously.

So what does qualify as an emergency? Medical bills, car repairs, unexpected or necessary expenses for the kids, unexpected bills, a job loss, etc. The key word is *unexpected*—things that aren't part of your normal monthly expenses, but that you definitely must pay.

As for new furniture, household items, etc.—these are purchases you plan for. As long as you have something to sit on, you don't *need* new furniture. But if you *want* new furniture, save for it and buy it with cash.

What Happens When You Dip Into It

Don't feel bad when you have to dip into your emergency fund. That's what it's there for. Many people are discouraged when they actually have to cover a financial emergency. While we all wish we could avoid them, they're a part of life! Instead, be thankful that you have some money saved and work toward replenishing the account.

It's key to be disciplined about putting the money back. This means you do the same thing you did to fund it in the first place, i.e., work extra jobs find something to sell and put all extra money into the account until you're back at your goal.

More Money-Making Ideas!

- Baby-sitting
- Senior citizen care: cooking, cleaning, transporting, etc.
- Have a garage sale. Maybe get together with some friends and have one.
- Tutor students in a subject you excel in, e.g., math, science, essay writing, etc.
- Landscaping and lawn care
- Pet-sit for neighbors on vacation or walk dogs.
- Become a virtual assistant for business owners. Check out www. elance.com or www.odesk.com.
- Participate in focus groups and market research. Visit http:// findfocusgroups.com/.
- Detail cars.
- Good with computers? Teach seniors the basics.
- Typing service
- Plant a garden and sell your produce.
- Sell baked goods to neighbors or at a local farmers market and during holidays.
- Write an e-book and sell it online.
- Garage clean up service
- Website design, graphic design, flyers, posters
- Are you artistic? Create paintings/drawings/poetry and sell them.
- Are you musically inclined? Not only can you sing or play an instrument at weddings and other events, you can also teach students/adults who want to learn.

Action Steps: Your List of Five!

1. List five spending habits you can cut in order to save for your emergency fund.

2. List five things you can do to earn extra money.

3. Go through each room of your home and look for at least five things you can sell. Don't forget the garage and basement.

4. Every day for five days, work on a strategy for adding money to your emergency fund. At the end of a work week, you should have a plan!

5. Encourage yourself five times per day by saying something positive about your financial future!

Congratulations! You are on your way! I'd love to hear about your progress! Shoot me a message any time at dorethia@themoneychat.com!

The Cordaways – Emergency Fund Hijacked by the Unexpected

With a family of four, my husband and I each kept an eye on the finances. What we needed was a system, a written plan, and more of a financial cushion. We would start our emergency fund, but weren't able to increase it because of unexpected expenses. We reached out to Dorethia to help us tighten up our budgeting, especially for inconsistent miscellaneous expenses.

It seemed that our money on miscellaneous items was going into a black hole. We were good with shopping for groceries and clothes and paying the mortgage since they were a set amount each month. It was the small things that came up that caused problems and threw our budget out of whack. We would try to pay for them quickly without looking into other deals or calling around. This behavior prevented us from saving as much as we wanted to.

For instance, when the need for a new musical instrument came up, we decided to rent. Done, right?

Well, not exactly. Dorethia showed us how buying a used one at a reasonable price was much smarter financially. On another occasion, my kids needed routine physicals and lab work. In order to get both services done by our doctor, I ended up paying for the lab work, which would have been free had I gone to another location to have it done. That was a needless expense in the name of convenience.

Working with Dorethia was very eye opening. As she helped us match our behaviors and spending habits with the numbers, we realized what was stopping us from reaching our goals. We developed a fund for unexpected, irregular expenses and added a line item in our budget to account for them and our emergency fund. We are now better able to forecast those expenses throughout the year and know how much extra we can put toward savings each month.

If the money isn't there, we wait. Even if we have it, we often still wait to ensure we aren't spending unnecessarily and not getting the biggest bang for our buck.

Growing Your Money

CHAPTER 7

Investing

#MoneyChat

"It's not how much money you make but how much money you keep, how hard it works for you and how many generations you keep it for."

ROBERT KIYOSAKI

WHEN YOU INVEST, YOU ARE taking the extra money from your account and making it work for you. Investment options can be as simple as signing up for a 401(k), putting a few dollars into stocks and bonds or buying a few shares of a mutual fund. At its core, investing is the process of allowing someone else to use your money in return for a share of their profit. Your open investment accounts are considered your investment 'portfolio'. If you only have a company pension, that is what your entire portfolio consists of. Some may have a mix of stocks, bonds, mutual funds and IRAs, etc.

Risk is involved in every investment. The general rule of thumb is that the higher the risk, the greater the return. Though investing is not technically considered gambling, you do have the potential to lose your money. This is why careful consideration and deliberate planning are important; so you can steadily grow your wealth and live comfortably on those investments.

Why Invest?

Life is unpredictable. You never know what's going to happen next, but you do know that it's most likely going to require money. Having funds set aside that are growing helps secure your financial future. Some are intimidated by investing because they don't understand it, don't know where to start or may not believe they'll ever have enough to invest. Then there are those who remember the stock market crashes and economic downturns where many people lost everything. All are very valid concerns, but not enough to keep you out of the game. As with anything, the stock market has its 'seasons' and it is based on what is going on in the world. You have to take the steps necessary to educate yourself on how it works so that you can benefit from the good (earning interest on your money) that it offers. No worries, you can learn bit by bit and I have outlined a primer to help—keep reading!

Portfolio

Your open investment accounts are considered your 'portfolio'. It could be a mix of any investment option, stocks, bonds, mutual funds, CDs, etc.

(** Mutual funds and retirement fund accounts are collections of stocks and bonds sold as packages, this is discussed more in the next section that outlines basic investing types.)

When Should I Add Investing to My Financial Life?

Investing is an advanced step in your financial plan. Answer these questions:

- I have a handle on my monthly expenses and pay my bills in entirety each month.
  ☐ **Yes** ☐ **No**

- There is money left over at the end of each month.
  ☐ **Yes** ☐ **No**

- I have paid off small debts and started paying off big debts.
  ☐ **Yes** ☐ **No**

If you did not say Yes to all of these, you should postpone investing outside of your employer retirement account until you can. I don't believe you have to be out of debt before you begin investing, especially if you are 35 or older, but I do believe in getting on a solid financial ground first.

Where Do You Start?

Great investment strategies start with a plan. The plan depends on your age, how much money you have to invest, your financial goals and the level of risk you're willing to take.

Here is a suggested roadmap, again, tweak it based on your needs and disposable income, but this gives you an idea:

1. **401K** Start here, once you are contributing at least 10–15% then…

2. **Mutual Fund**, once you have 1 or 2, add a

3. **Roth IRA** to your portfolio … and keep building from there.

As your disposable income increases, you can open more mutual fund and Roth IRA accounts. Then once you believe you are a knowledgeable investor, possibly buy some stocks via a discount broker like Etrade or Sharebuilder. It is key to continue to increase your investing goals and to have additional accounts outside of your employer retirement account or pension.

How Much Do You Need?

That is the million-dollar question. You are in control of your wealth and, while anyone can offer you wealth management tips, you are the one who decides what goes where. That's why it's so important to have a realistic picture of your current finances and to know what you're building wealth for. Begin with the end in mind and that will help you estimate how much you'll need. Do you want to supplement your retirement? Build a dream home one day? Start a business? Many want to pass money down to their children and grandchildren. Maybe you have a goal of being a millionaire one day. It is all achievable.

When you're going to need the money will determine the type of investment you choose. In other words, if you have 20 years, you may choose a type of IRA, whereas if you only have a couple of years, a mutual fund or CD may be better. Having these numbers at your disposal will also help you figure out how much you need to invest.

RISK: Don't Put All Your Eggs in One Basket

The best way to defer the potential risks of your investments is through diversification. I know, we hear about this all the time. It's no big deal really; it only means having more than one type of investment. Spreading your investments around in multiple areas gives you the cushion to brace yourself if one investment fails, you still have others that can support your financial goals. No matter how excellent an investment vehicle seems to be, there's always the chance that things can go awry and you'll lose money.

Investing on a Budget

If you want to tip your toe in and start with a small amount of money just to apply what you are learning you can use a discount broker to open a brokerage account. Sound fancy? It's not a big deal, really. A brokerage account is simply an account that allows you to buy and sell investments. It's a little like opening a bank account, you're just doing it with a brokerage firm. Here, we are discussing online brokerage accounts that allow you to begin investing with very little money vs. traditional brokerage accounts.

*Retirement accounts are also considered 'brokerage' accounts; we discuss those in Chapter 9.

Diversification Example 1:

Let's take Kevin for example, he is a nurse at a local hospital and has the following investments portfolio:

- Employer 401k
- Mutual fund focused on growth
- Stock in two tech companies
- Stock in one health-care company
- 10 Bonds – many received as gifts

Diversification Example 2:

Another version of diversification is based on the stocks held in your mutual fund or retirement account. You don't want to have a mutual fund or retirement account that only invests in all tech stocks because if the technology industry fails, you will take a huge loss. Instead, you want to have a mix of various industries.

Craig has $3,000 to invest, which he saved from his tax return. He chose to put $2,000 in a mutual fund that represented various industries he was interested in. This fund included a balanced percentage of the following types of stocks: technology, healthcare, consumer staples and financial services. If Craig were to put the entire $2,000 in a fund heavy in any one of those areas, he would lose money if that fund took a dip. Because he has diversified, his investment should remain stable. And the remaining $1,000? Since he already has an emergency fund, he opened an IRA separate from the 401(k) he has with his employer. His plan is to direct deposit $100 per month into both his IRA and his mutual fund.

So now when you hear the financial gurus on television talking about 'portfolio diversification', you know exactly what they are talking about!

Action Steps: Ask Yourself a Few Questions

There are a few things to consider when deciding where to invest:

1. What are you comfortable with? Are you generally more conservative or are you willing to bet the farm?

2. How much money can you afford to lose without losing sleep? There's nothing wrong with taking risks as long as you understand your limits and know when to make adjustments. If you watch every penny, you may want to opt for safer investments that grow income slower.

3. Based on your age and when you'll need to access your money, what is the best mix of investments for you? A younger person can generally take more risks because they have more time to accumulate wealth.

Once you consider your risk, it's time to visit your financial advisor. This leads us to...

How to Choose a Financial Advisor

Financial advisors are needed and there are many who are excellent at their job. One way to find one for your finances is to ask family and friends for references. LinkedIN is also a good way to find professionals. Some advisors have free workshops or may be guest speakers in the community. I like these type of events because you can get to know them in a sense before doing business with them.

Pick at least three to five to consider, and meet with each of them. Planners have to file an ADV Form Part II with the Securities and Exchange Commission (SEC) which shows their services, background, and fees. Most will automatically share this form with you, but if not you can ask for it. States also have records on each financial advisor, you can check with the securities regulator in your state for complaints and to ensure they are licensed. Also if they are a member of the National Association of Personal Financial Advisors (NAPFA) www.napfa.org, they don't receive commissions or other incentives for selling or recommending particular investment products.

Everyone who meets with a financial advisor should:

1. Have educated yourself on basic investing concepts like those found in this chapter
2. Know how much money you want to invest
3. Know what you want the advisor to do for you and be able to tell them
4. Ask for references
5. Have questions prepared, such as: How long have they been an advisor, What is their main area of focus, why are they suggesting a particular route for you, etc.

Pay attention to the advisor, are they listening to what you are saying your goals are, are they asking you questions about yourself or are they simply telling you what you should do or what they think is best. Don't get me wrong, they are there to advise you and you need be open to their suggestions. That said, they should be able to tell you clearly how their solutions line up with your stated goals. You should never feel pushed into a saving or investing direction you are not comfortable with.

Never buy at the first meeting. Go home, think about your options and then make a decision. Don't feel like you are bugging the advisor if you have to call with questions after the meeting, that is what they are there for and most don't mind.

Types of Accounts

Brokerage

A **traditional brokerage** account gives you access to the advice and expertise of a stock broker. Companies like Edward Jones and UBS are traditional brokerage firms. Your broker will give you financial advice, portfolio reports and can be reached very easily. They will also offer research materials and explain them to help guide your investment decisions. These types of services can be very expensive and charge high commission rates, but if you're looking for the ease associated with having someone else handle your investment decisions, this is the way to go. This higher level of service also results in faster turn-around times for each trade. Most traditional brokerage accounts have minimum deposit requirements and charge fees on your account if it is below a certain amount. These fees will eat into your investments early on, especially if you're just beginning

Discount brokerage firms also have brokers, but they only handle the nuts and bolts of trades. There's generally an online system that account holders will use to buy and sell orders and the brokers on the other end handle the rest, no questions asked. It may be difficult to actually talk to a broker if you have one of these accounts. Because this type of service is more DIY (do it yourself), you pay significantly lower commissions. The amount of research and the tools available to discount brokerage account holders has been improving.

Certificates of Deposit

Certificates of Deposit are very secure investments in that you are guaranteed to get the amount you invested back plus interest once the CD matures. The interest rates are low though, maybe a little more than an money market or interest bearing checking or saving account. There are varying types of CD accounts and a visit to your local bank can help you determine which one may be right for you. *Types of CDs:*

Traditional

This is the original old school CD. You deposit a certain amount for a certain term and earn interest. If you withdraw before the term is up you will pay hefty penalties, but you are able to add money to the CD during the term.

Bump-up

If you buy a CD and then see the rate goes up, you can 'bump up' to that higher rate for the rest of your CDs term. Generally, you can do this once during the life of the CD.

Liquid

With this type you are able to withdraw without penalty, but the money must stay in the account at least 7 days. There may also be a limit on the number of withdrawals you can make. Of course the interest rate is lower than other CDs, that aren't so liquid.

Zero-coupon

A zero-coupon CD is bought at a discount, (think groupon), but you are paid face value upon maturity. For example you may pay $10,000 for a CD valued at $20,000. Though you don't earn interest on these type of CDS, you are paid the full value of $20,000 upon its maturity.

Individual Retirement Accounts (IRAs)

This type of account is perfect for those who aren't offered an employer plan, are looking to save more for retirement or want to follow my advice of stashing away money for retirement separate from your employer account. There are traditional IRAs (before tax contributions) and Roth IRAs (after-tax contributions) These are discussed in detail in Chapter 9 on retirement.

Your Employer

The easiest way to start investing is to participate in your employer-sponsored retirement account. This is often a 401(k), 403(b), 457 or governmental TSP account. These accounts generally use a combination of mutual funds, stocks and bonds to spread out risk. While some employers have dropped this benefit since the economic downturn, many will still pay in matching funds at either a percentage or an equal match to what you contribute to the fund. Over time, your fund grows and doesn't get taxed until you withdraw your money. We talk about these types of accounts in depth in our Retirement Chapter 9.

Many like to have at least $1,000 when opening a brokerage account. But no worries if you'd like to start with less, most discount brokerages have no or low account minimum requirements.

Types of Investments

We've all heard triumphant stories about investors being at the right place at the right time and making millions in the market. We've also heard tragic stories about how investors have lost millions of dollars on bad investment decisions. For those of you who are new to investing, it can seem like a huge minefield of good and bad decisions and opinions. While there are risks in making investments, it's still an opportunity to prepare for your future and set yourself up for life. There are a number of ways to invest and you can start small and slow to ease into it.

Bonds

Government bonds (including federal, state, and local) and corporate bonds (from large companies) are considered safe investments when compared to stocks and mutual funds. The entity that issues bonds asks for your investment. In return for your investment, the bonds offer you a small amount of guaranteed interest after a certain period of time.

You might receive a one-year bond at 1% from a company. That company is guaranteeing that when the bond matures, it will give you your investment back, plus 1%. The percentage rates on bonds are usually very low because the issuing entity cannot predict the movement of the market and other areas, and doesn't know exactly how much interest it will really earn on its investments.

Stocks

Over the last 85 years, stocks have generally outperformed most other investment alternatives. According to Ibbotson Associates, an institutional investment advisory firm, stocks have gone up an average of 10.4% over the past 90 years. When you purchase a stock, what you're doing is purchasing a very small piece of ownership in a particular company. As stocks are traded back and forth, the market decides just how much each piece of stock is worth that day. To purchase stocks, an investor will almost always work through a brokerage firm.

Before deciding which stocks to buy, consider how risk averse you are and how much time you have to hold on to the investment. If you are very risk averse, going with long-term, proven stocks, such as utilities and other large, well-established corporations, are your best bet. If you're after potentially larger and quicker profits in your investment portfolio, then riskier stocks in rapid growth areas may be right for you.

Mutual Funds

Instead of owning a single stock or bond, mutual funds are collections of stocks and bonds sold as packages. Investors mutually pool their money and invest in shares of this fund. The money made from mutual funds is then redistributed in the form of dividends based on the amount of money that was put into the fund.

> *Dividends… If an investment earns a certain amount of profit, some of that profit (cash) is then paid out to the shareholders quarterly or annually.*

One of the largest advantages this type of investment offers is a lower cost per entry. Since a mutual fund pools together money from various sources, one person doesn't have to carry the entire load of the mutual fund itself. It's diversified to the point where there's not as much risk involved.

There are costs associated with the administration and management of a mutual fund that we will discuss later. Costs are added because there are a lot of moving parts within a fund. Did you know that someone still has to purchase the individual securities and bonds and then make the separate investment to group all of them together?

Where to Open an Account

1. **Brokerage Firm** – facilitates the purchase of all investments

2. **Financial Advisor** – works with a brokerage firm to purchase your investments

3. **Banks** – works with a brokerage firm the same as a financial advisor would

4. **Directly** – you can buy investments directly, but this is suggested for the savvy investor only. Beginning investors should get professional help when purchasing until they are more knowledgeable and have done extensive research

There are a lot of good brokerage firms out there and it is becoming more and more popular to purchase via a discount online brokerage firm. Now they are called discount because there are less fees, but also remember you won't receive that gold amenities either. Many are okay with this because they feel they are getting a bigger bang for their buck. Every time you make a trade there's normally some sort of fee that goes along with it, but you aren't paying as much as you do with traditional brokerage firms. Here are some of the most popular and their terms/fees as of the writing of this book:

- **E*Trade:** E*Trade was one of the first online brokerages to offer every type of investment and they're still a market leader. They require no account minimums and charge no account service fees. E*Trade charges a standard $9.99 per stock and options trade with varying rates for other investments. They also offer a full suite of research tools at no cost.

- **Sharebuilder:** Sharebuilder tries to distinguish itself as the lowest cost choice for long-term buy-and-hold investors. This is because they offer an automated investing plan with commissions of only $4 per trade. They also have no account minimums and charge no service fees. However, if you decide to change investments or invest outside the automated plan, you'll pay $9.95 per trade. Sharebuilder also offers research tools, but not as many as E*Trade.

- **Fidelity:** Fidelity was initially only a full-service brokerage but has grown to become an online leader over the last few years. They offer every type of account and investment, but many people opt for their traditional accounts and low prices. There are no annual fees if you maintain an account minimum of $2,500 and their minimum deposit requirement is $2,500 for most accounts. They also have a standard $7.95 commission on all stock trades.

When opening a brokerage account, it's always best to investigate all of your options and match your investment strategy to the level of interaction you wish to have with the account. These discount options are very good if you want to try your hand at doing the research and making the investments yourself. But a full-service brokerage or a financial advisor might be the best choice if you don't wish to be concerned with the day-to-day movement of your money.

How to Research Companies to Invest In

We discussed that mutual funds and stocks all have 'ticker' symbols; you can research their historical and projected performance on financial websites such as Morningstar and Yahoo finance. In addition to researching how much money they may make you, you will also want to check for any negative or positive media about company stock or mutual fund. For company stock, is the CEO in the media? Has there been any product recalls or other happenings that may cause stock price to dip? You will want a mutual fund that has had consistent returns of 8 -12% over an 8 – 12 year period. Choose one where the fund manager has been in place for 10 years or more. You can research they types of industries and companies that are in your mutual fund accounts to determine if there are any current events that may affect the funds performance as well.

Action Steps: Time to Do Some Reading!

1. **Website:**

   - *The Motley Fool* – www.fool.com
     I have followed this website since its inception many years ago! It is perfect for learning many areas of finance including help for the beginning or advanced investor. Start with the 'How to Invest 101' series. Investopedia.com is also another good website.

2. **Books:**

   - *Investing Success* – Lynnette Khalfani - Excellent advice for new investors

   - *The Little Book of Common Sense Investing* – John C. Bogle – This is an eye-opening view of creating wealth by investing in index funds. Definitely a must read before investing.

3. **Magazines:**

   - I love Black Enterprise and Money Magazines. They both provide financial insight regardless of where you are on this money journey.

Wait a Minute. We are Talking about Investing. What about Annuities?

Annuities are investment vehicles that provide a guaranteed payment for a specific period of time, i.e., 10 to 20 years or the rest of your life. To put it in perspective, we're all familiar with social security and pensions, right? Well those are also types of annuities—they're just offered by the government or your employer. Individuals can also buy their own annuity from an investment advisor or insurance company.

Fixed Annuities

Fixed annuities give you fixed payments over the life (time frame) of the annuity. In the case of the social security system or the pension system, that fixed payment amount is dependent upon the amount of money you've put in and your expected lifespan. (Insurance people have amazingly detailed tables to determine this information.)

Let's say you have $50,000 to put into an annuity, and you want to get an annuity that will give you a payment for the rest of your life, which you expect to be 15 more years. You would buy a 15-year annuity that would give you around $277 each month.

The math:

$50,000/15 years = $3,333 per year
$3,333/12 months = $277.00 per month

Variable Annuities

Variable annuities give you fluctuating payments over the life of the annuity. Payments amounts are based on the investments inside the annuity, your expected lifespan, and how much money you have invested.

For example, if you put that same $50,000 in a variable annuity, you would receive your $277 as a minimum, but it could also be more since payments fluctuate.

Guaranteed Annuities

There is often concern over what happens to an annuity in case you die. A guaranteed annuity ensures payouts even in the event of the annuity owner's death. Payments would go to your estate.

Joint Annuities

Joint annuities can be passed on from person to person in the event of your death. This works in cases where you want to make sure your spouse is "taken care of" on your passing. Usually, the payments are lower, but a guaranteed payment is still being made.

Pros and Cons of Investing in Annuities

Pros

The biggest incentive to setting up an annuity is the automatic payments you receive each month for the rest of your life. This provides a budgeting foundation and gives you a little more peace of mind. This is key during retirement years or in the case of a medical concern that doesn't allow you to work.

If you haven't quite gotten a handle on your financial habits, the money is out of your hands with no opportunity to blow it and have nothing to show for it later.

Cons

Before establishing a personal annuity, make sure that it is the right investment vehicle for you. Once you've invested in an annuity, it's nearly impossible to withdraw the money—annuities are designed to be irrevocable. Getting your money back usually involves very costly surrender charges.

The money you receive from your annuity is also not adjusted for inflation. Two hundred dollars now may be great, but that same amount 10 years from now might only get you a stick of gum.

There is also a cost for setting up and administering the annuity. In many cases, you can pay up to two to three percent of the value of your investment every year. These payments drive down the overall value of the investment.

As with any investment, do your homework before choosing an annuity and talk with your financial advisor or insurance agent to discuss your options.

CHAPTER 8

Digging Deeper

#MoneyChat

You don't have to be a genius to invest well.

WARREN BUFFET

OF COURSE, I COULDN'T WRITE about investing and not quote Warren Buffet! I like this quote because I believe it wholeheartedly. Take baby steps, learn the rules and win the game! Class is in session! Throughout this chapter, I will be telling you to do your homework, to do your research, at the end of it I tell you how!

Here we will take a deep dive—equipping you with the information needed to invest wisely!

More About Stocks

When people think of investing, the first thing that probably comes to mind is a stock. The state of the stock market is a daily news item and the Dow Jones Industrial Average (aka DJIA or The DOW) is an accepted barometer of how well the economy is doing.

While the market is complex, the basics are simple. A single share of stock represents the smallest amount of ownership you can have in a company and when you buy a stock, you're buying a very tiny portion of the company. People with a lot of stock in a company can influence it through shareholder meetings, but that will come later. What's more important to know at this point is how stocks make money for you. There are two main methods.

Buy Low/Sell High

The first method is buying a stock when its price is low and selling it when its price is high. To look up the cost of a stock or, to use investing terminology, its *share price*, you'll need to find out two things:

- Which *exchange* the stock is traded on
- The stock's *ticker symbol*. This can be searched for at http:// finance.yahoo.com/

When you look at the newspaper listings for a stock, you'll normally get three pieces of information:

- The price of the stock at the end of the trading day before
- The amount by which its price went up or down over the course of that day
- The percent by which its price has changed

Looking at Amazon as I write this, I see that it's trading at $254.23 and that it's down $3.85, or 1.51%. But that's just its relative change during the day. Stocks are really a long-term game. Most people suggest holding on to a share of stock for about two to three years before trying to sell it off.

Amazon is traded on the NASDAQ exchange and its ticker symbol is AMZN. Over a five-day spread, a share of Amazon stock rose from $249.27 to $258.05. So if you bought a single share of stock on the first day of the five-day spread and sold it four days later, you would have made $8.78 ($258.05 - $249.27). This may not seem like much and you're right. However, if you bought this share of Amazon stock back in May of 2008 when its price was $77.31, selling it at the end of our five-day spread would have yielded $180.74. That's not a bad return *and* that's only one share!

Now if the stock had gone in the other direction, you would have lost money when you sold it. This is why investing is a calculated risk. Do you sell off the stock now and eat your loss before its price goes down any further, or do you hold on to it and pray that its price goes up again, and that it goes up enough to make it profitable? This is why you must research companies before you buy their stock; so you can judge whether or not they'll be profitable over time. Companies that report regular profits and growth in their quarterly earnings reports are seen as more valuable, and this pushes the stock price up. Companies that don't perform as well in their quarterly earnings are somewhat devalued and their stock's price goes down. This is why earnings reports are so eagerly reported in financial news.

> **Earnings reports** *are simply financial reports companies publish quarterly to show how strong their company is financially. Did they make a profit? If so, how much? If not, why and do they expect to do better next quarter?*

By spreading your investment capital (money) over multiple stocks, you can absorb price fluctuations a lot easier. "Blue chip" stocks make a great first investment in the stock market. These are the stocks of companies that are very well established and are very unlikely to collapse, though nothing's impossible.

Dividends

The other way that stocks make money for you is through dividends. When a company makes a profit, it can decide to pay some of that profit directly to its shareholders. The amount you get depends on how much stock you own, how much stock is out there for that company, and how much of the profit the shareholders vote to pay out as dividends. Some companies pay quarterly dividends, others yearly and some not at all. For most beginning investors, dividends are a sort of bonus that happens on occasion.

More About Mutual Funds

One of the problems with diversification is a lack of capital... aka cash! Many beginning investors aren't able to spread out their money enough to be safe in investing. Mutual funds came about as a way to get around this problem. In a mutual fund, your money is pooled with other people's money. The company managing the fund then invests that money into many different kinds of investments.

If you have any sort of retirement account, like a 401(k) or a Roth IRA, you probably have investments in one or more mutual funds already. When you look over the different "plans" you can invest in through a 401(k), most of them are mutual funds of one kind or another. When you invest in a mutual fund, you get shares—much like stock—that signify what portion of the holdings in the fund belong to you.

How do you earn money from mutual funds?

- Dividends on stocks and interest on bonds

- Selling investments the fund holds that have increased in price

- The shares of the mutual fund themselves increase in price, which can then be sold by you

Now, you can receive a check for the money earned or you have the option to reinvest to buy more shares. The latter is the suggested strategy; remember investing should be a long-term journey. You cut yourself short if you cash in earnings.

The advantages of a mutual fund are ease of diversification and their *liquidity* (how easy it is to access your money). You are able to close the account and pocket your money whenever you choose without any penalties.

Alright, hold on tight—there are many different types of mutual funds:

- **Money market funds** invest in *short-term debt instruments*. These are very safe. You can't lose your *principal* (initial investment) with these. However, their rate of return is very low, about as good as a certificate of deposit (CD).

- **Bond funds** – The goal of these funds is to provide a steady income to all their investors through investing in the bond market. These are great for conservative investors, but there's still risk involved and you are subject to bond interest rate fluctuations.

- **Equity funds** (Stocks) – This is the largest category of mutual funds, they invest in stocks and are divided into 'classes' dependent on:

  1. The size of the company (small, mid-size or large) in terms of how much capital (money) they have.

  2. How risky those companies' investments are (value, growth or blend).

     a. Value – may be undervalued in that the stock may be trading at a lower price than the company is actually worth. Focus is on safety rather than growth so the investing strategy is not as aggressive.

     b. Growth – riskier, but also have better returns, these companies are expected to have faster growth and earnings potential than others.

     c. Blend – you guessed it, a combination of the two.

- **Balanced funds** – are a mix of stocks and bonds, the idea is provide some level of safety and income diversifying the two types of investments.

- **Global or International funds** – At first glance, you would think these meant the same thing right? Nope. A global fund invests in foreign stocks that do not include your home country. International funds invest in foreign stocks, but could include your home country. Some are wary of investing in foreign stocks, but you just have to do your homework as with anything else. You will face risks based on the country, politics, etc., but do your research. These types of funds are good for diversifying your portfolio and depending on the countries represented, may provide the returns you desire.

- **Index Funds** – Invests in companies based on the market indexes such as Standard & Poors (S&P) 500 or Dow Jones Industrial Average (DJIA). These funds have lower fees than regular mutual funds and you don't have to pay brokerage commissions.

- **Exchange Traded Funds** – Also follows the indexes, trades like regular stock on an exchange and you have to pay brokerage commissions. Prices fluctuate throughout the day as they are bought and sold.

- **Specialty Funds** – Invests in companies within the same:
  Sector – technology, healthcare, finance, etc.
  Region – certain countries or geographical areas
  Socially responsible – may not invest in things that are against beliefs such as alcohol, weapons, cigarettes, etc.

Mutual Fund Fees

Of course, the people running the funds need to eat and so there are fees involved with mutual funds. There are two main types of fees: a *MER* and a *load*.

Management Expense Ratio (MER), is the fee for managing the fund and is calculated as a percentage of the fund's assets. The average rate is between 0.2% and 1.5%. Higher fees don't necessarily mean that you'll get a better rate on return. Unfortunately, this is the price you pay in the mutual fund game and you'll have to watch your statements carefully to make sure you're getting a good return on your mutual fund investment.

Capital Gains Taxes!

You will have to pay taxes on the dividends you receive at the end of the year. Talk to an accountant and a financial advisor about capital gains taxes and your mutual fund investments.

Loads are fees taken from you to pay the salespeople for selling you the fund. It's basically their commission. The beginning investor should avoid any fund with a load. There are plenty of no-load (no fee) mutual funds and they often out-perform those with fees.

When you go to a broker, a bank or a mutual fund website, you'll need to know a few things.

Net Asset Value (NAV), of the mutual fund. This is how much you'll need to pay to buy a share in the fund. It's much like the share price of a stock.

Second, you should know how much risk you're willing to endure, how much money you want to invest and whether you want to do it all at once or over time. All of this information will help your financial planner decide which funds to show you.

You can also use a service like Morningstar.com to help search through funds and get their rankings and current information about them. In fact, the Internet is the best place to learn about funds now. You can get a long-term analysis of a fund to see its performance over time, which will be the best thing for an initial investor. Save day trading for the experts who can stomach it!

Whew! Okay, take a deep breath. I know it is a lot to take in, but you are doing fine! Next, we're going to dip into the last major area of investing—the bond market.

More About Bonds

Compared to the exciting volatility of the stock market, bonds may seem boring. However, bonds are an extremely important part of the economy and a safe place to put your money long term if you do it correctly.

First, a bond is basically an I.O.U. If a corporation or government wants to fund operations or a special project, they can issue bonds to the public. Let's say you buy a $1,000 bond. One thousand dollars is the bond's *face value*. In exchange for your $1,000, the company issuing the bond (the *issuer*) promises to pay you yearly interest on it. This yearly interest is known as the *coupon*. The bond will pay interest until the length of the loan is up and the bond matures. The day this happens is called the *maturity date*. On that day, the issuer repays the investor the face value of the bond.

For example, if you buy a $5,000 bond at a 5% coupon for 10 years, you will receive $250 a year from the bond for 10 years, generally divided into two payments. At the end of 10 years, you'll get your $5,000 back and you'll have made a profit of $2,500 dollars.

The major difference between bonds and stocks is that bonds are considered debt for the issuer. If the issuer was to go belly up, the bondholders would get paid first from any liquidation. But with a bond you don't get any share of company ownership like you would with a stock. Nor would you get any additional benefits if the company did very well from your investment. Thus, bonds have a lower return than stocks in most instances.

Many retirees love bonds because their principal is secure no matter what happens. Bonds are a great way to provide a fixed income. They're also very good if you have a short-term goal that must have a stable source of income, such as education.

The risk from bonds comes from the creditworthiness of the company issuing them. It's just like any other loan. Can you expect the company to pay back the face value and all the interest owed when the bond matures? Credit rating companies like Moody's and

Fitch also rate the worthiness of bonds to show investors how good (or bad) the credit of a company is. A company whose bonds have a very low rating (called junk bonds) is much riskier to invest in, but you can get a very high coupon out of them. So-called *junk bonds* can be riskier than stocks.

Bonds come in several categories:

- *Bills* are bonds that mature in less than a year.

- *Notes* are bonds that mature between one and 10 years.

- *Bonds* (true bonds) mature after 10 years or longer

Bonds also differ by who issues them. U.S. government bonds are issued in all the types above, and are normally called T-bills/notes/bonds, short for Treasury. Because the U.S. is so stable, Treasury bonds are some of the safest investments out there. However, developing countries also issue bonds to fund infrastructure products and there's a lot of risk there. As recent financial crises have shown, countries can default just like companies can.

The cost for investing in Treasury securities is quite low, but the lower you go the fewer advantages you have. The normal minimum price you have to purchase to get a Treasury security is $1,000. However, there are special Savings Bonds that can be bought at lower rates and have a coupon! The two current types are EE Series bonds and I Series bonds. The minimum purchase price for these is $25 and you can buy up to $10,000 per social security number per year. You have to hold them for at least a year before you can cash them out. They must also be bought through TreasuryDirect.gov. For more information on Savings Bonds, check out https://www.treasurydirect.gov/indiv/research/indepth/ebonds/res_e_bonds_eecomparison.htm. If you're not ready to do major investing in standard Treasury securities then Savings Bonds are the way to go.

Municipal bonds are those issued by city governments allowing you to invest in that city. Depending on your bond and your relationship with the city, some of these bonds are tax-free. Municipal bonds can provide a significant savings on your investment. It is more likely that a city will go bankrupt before the federal government, but it would still be pretty rare. And, finally, there are corporate bonds, which are issued by companies. These have the highest yields because they're the most prone to risk. The normal minimum amount you need to purchase to get one is $5,000.

There are lower-priced options that have no coupon. Instead, you pay a cost lower than the face cost of the bond and get the full price of it at a later date. These are known as zero-coupon bonds, discount bonds, or deep discount bonds. These are not good for investment, but they are excellent if you need a specific amount of income at a later date. For example, if you know you want to have a certain amount of money for college for your child, you could by zero-coupon bonds. That way you wouldn't have to worry about fluctuating interest rates.

Within the bond market, sometimes also called the debt market, the credit market, or the fixed income market, you have two different types of purchasers. There's the market between the investors and the issuers, and there's the market made of people who are trading bonds back and forth among themselves. If you want to eventually trade bonds, rather than just hold them to maturity, I highly recommend you go through this short course on understanding and buying bonds at Investopedia.com. http://www.investopedia.com/university/bonds/

To buy a bond, just talk with any broker. Remember that you may need to meet minimum investment amounts to buy certain types of loans. You can also buy bonds directly from the issuer, especially government bonds. Remember, you can buy U.S. government bonds at www.treasurydirect.gov, which will have all the info you need to buy T-notes, T-bills, T-bonds, and savings bonds.

Key Points:

- Buying a bond is like giving a loan to the government or municipality. When it matures, or when you cash it in in the case of a savings bond, you get your principle (face value) plus interest (coupon payments) back.

- They are a very stable investment option. In fact, Treasury securities are considered to be one of the most stable investment options in the world.

- Treasury securities require a $1000 minimum investment. Municipal bonds require a $5000 minimum investment.

- Savings bonds (types EE and I) can be bought for as little as $25 each.

- To buy bonds, talk with a broker or go to TreasuryDirect.gov.

- Some bonds have no coupon. That means you pay a discount on the face value of the bond, then get the face value of the bond back at a later date. Not good for investing, but good for things like college tuition.

- Take the short Investopedia course mentioned above to get a deeper insight into the specifics of buying and trading bonds.

Bonus: Before We Say "I Do:" Couples and Investing

Financial Coach – LaKeisha Mallet

We are currently living in an age where being financially astute should be a way of life for all of us. Times have changed, dynamics in the home have changed and, many times, both partners in a relationship work outside of the home, just to make ends meet. Getting married, planning a wedding and deciding to share the rest of your life with the one you love is probably one of the most joyous occasions in a person's life. Finding that special someone and vowing to commit the rest of your life to loving and cherishing them, 'til death do you part, is not a task anyone should take lightly.

With fights about money and money problems being the number one cause of divorce, many couples get married not knowing that debt is a key destructive force that has ruined many marriages. Having a heart-to-heart discussion with the one you love about the state of your finances, and even your financial expectations, is not as sexy a topic as most lovers want to discuss, but I believe that if the hard financial questions are addressed before the nuptials, it will increase a couples' odds of 'til death do us part instead of 'til debt do us part.

Before I decided to say, "I do," I wanted to fully understand my partner's views on money, debt, savings, retirement, etc. I wanted to know if he had any financial goals and if any of his goals were aligned with things that were also important to me. One of the first questions I chose to ask my future husband was, "What drives your decisions with money?" And there were books that helped us engage in healthy communication concerning our current financial situations. One of those books was *The Hard Questions: 100 Questions to Ask Before Getting Engaged* by Susan Piver.

The Hard Questions addressed many of the necessary topics a couple should discuss in any premarital session. It urged couples to discuss the expectations they had for their marriage, to examine how those expectations differed and to find some common ground regarding those differences. Topics included things like where to live, whether to have children or adopt, how close is too close for the in-laws and, of course, the topic dearest to me—*money*. The book gave detailed questions to ask your potential spouse about how they viewed money and I used those questions to help determine whether Jeff and I would thrive together financially.

I asked Jeff questions like how much debt he had and if there was a plan to pay it off. That question was easy for me to answer because I had achieved debt freedom early in our dating relationship. I also asked him whether his dream home was in the big city or the suburbs. Was sending his children to private school an option—from a financial perspective? Or would public education be the best choice? We went on to discuss how much money we each had in our checking and savings accounts and if we were aggressively stashing cash for a rainy day.

From there the conversation turned to investing. We discussed our investing philosophies and I discovered that I'm more of a conservative investor while Jeff has his own brokerage accounts and is quite an aggressive investor. At this realization, we decided that after the wedding we would continue to invest as we had but create a joint portfolio that would be a mix of our different investing styles.

As we coach couples about money, we always stress the importance of being on the same page and being in agreement. No two people are exactly alike and neither will their philosophies on money and investing be. It's vital that each partner voices their needs from a personal finance perspective and is clear about what their financial goals are and how they wish to achieve them.

My husband likes to dabble in day trading. I think it's too risky and not a wise investment move. However, outside of our savings and the investments we share, and after we take care of all of our responsibilities, any money left over goes to Jeff for him to invest. That was important for us to decide in advance so that in the event Jeff's stocks don't perform as well as he hopes, I won't have to give him the evil eye for blowing money we need. We urge each partner to understand their risk tolerance level and the role it will play in their approach to investing as a married couple. It's so important for couples to learn to communicate their financial desires and plans long before they decide on wedding colors, caterers and flowers.

I believe all couples should have "the talk"—how to invest, when to invest and where to invest (outside of 401(k)s and IRAs). The couples we coach often wonder if they should have joint investments. While that's a personal preference, I'm a firm believer in the art of communication. Each spouse is responsible for understanding the financial affairs of the unit and for being aware of how the money in every account is changing from month to month each quarter. Couples must also reach a mutual agreement as to when it is necessary to increase the amount they invest.

With regard to buying stocks, another decision couples need to make is when to buy, sell and hold. There will likely be times when one partner wants to buy and the other wants to sell. There has to have been a discussion about how to handle situations when you disagree about money. This strategy works for other areas in the relationship as well. When discussing any piece of the financial equation with your partner, only do what you feel comfortable doing because you have to be able to sleep at night. If investing 75% of your retirement account in stocks will cause you anxiety then opt for a more conservative investment strategy. Whatever you decide, you have to be comfortable with the decision.

Once a couple has decided to marry their finances, it's imperative that they discuss when and for what reasons they will ever touch their invested money. I don't believe couples should touch their retirement savings for any reason, especially not to make major purchases. The penalties for withdrawing funds prematurely are too high. However, we do advise couples to have a particular fund that they regularly contribute to; an interest-bearing account that eventually will grow to a point where they can live off its interest.

After debt has been eliminated and long-term savings are in place, we advise our clients to save 10% of their take-home pay each month to put toward an "in case we need it" account. I like the term "in case we need it" for things that are not necessarily an emergency but are still unexpected or unanticipated.

Help your spouse stay on track with their financial goals. Make it fun and make it rewarding. When you reach a goal or major financial milestone, celebrate! Making money and watching it grow should be fun and easy. Take the stress out of discussing money by approaching it as equal partners who will one day enjoy the fruits of your joint labor. Who better to enjoy life on the beaches of the world with than your spouse? By talking about your finances early and often, you'll eventually have the money to do it.

LAKEISHA MALLETT, MBA, ONE HALF of the dynamic duo of Mallett Coaching, is a trained Personal Finance Coach. She is known for her coaching philosophy "Saying I DO...It's about Love and Money too!!" LaKeisha, along with her husband Jeff, empower couples with their practical financial knowledge to have happier relationships and attain lasting financial results by creating a personalized step-by-step spending plans to achieve their financial goals.

Connect with LaKeisha!
Visit: www.mallettcoaching.com
Twitter @mallettcoaching
IG: @keishamallett

CHAPTER 9

Retirement

Many people take no care of their money 'til they come nearly to the end of it, and others do just the same with their time.

JOHANN WOLFGANG VON GOETHE

N A SURVEY CONDUCTED BY *The Employee Benefit Research Institute,* only 14% of people were confident they'd have enough money in retirement. What about you? Do you think you'll have enough? Do you have dreams about lazy days by the pool or nightmares about living out of a cardboard box?

How Much Will You Need?

Do the math. Can you live on less than your income or will you want it to stay the same? Realistically, most people want to keep the same lifestyle in retirement. If you earn $60,000 now, do you really want to live on $40,000 in retirement? Be honest with yourself and calculate the true amount you'd like to work with each year. For those who may have to care for their parents or their grandchildren, it would be wise to include an estimate of those annual costs as well. As we age, our healthcare costs rise. There may be more doctor visits, prescriptions and, possibly, hospitalizations. It's better to face the possibility than be unprepared when the time comes. But on a more upbeat note—add travel! You've worked hard all your life and you should enjoy yourself, so be sure to throw in some money for travel!

Seriously consider how you can get rid of debt using the strategies I've outlined in Sections 1: Getting Out of the Hole and Section 2: Getting on Solid Ground in the years leading up to your retirement. You want to enter retirement with the least amount of debt possible and a sure financial footing.

When Should You Start?

It's ideal to begin saving for retirement from the moment you start your first job, but we all know it doesn't quite work out that way for many of us. Therefore, when you start will depend on your income, expenses, goals and age. Here are some rules of thumb you may be able to apply to your situation:

Minimal debt? Money left each month after bills are paid? The sky's the limit! Contribute the maximum of 15% and take advantage of the full match from your employer. If you aren't quite ready to contribute 15%, start where you can (ideally, at least 6%) and build up over time. Some employers may require you to put in a certain percent before they'll match your savings. If so, put in at least that amount. You can contribute less, you just won't receive the match.

Loads of debt? Press pause on any retirement savings. I'd say don't contribute until you at least pay down some of your smaller debts.

If you're in your 20s and 30s and have a lot of debt, you still have time to focus on getting rid of it over the next few years. You can start saving for retirement once you've become financially stable and still pay off debt. After you've gotten rid of a large chunk of your outstanding debts, you'll be able to contribute more money to your retirement when you do start again.

If you are past the age of 40 and have a large amount of debt, focus on eliminating as much debt as possible over the next two to three years. After that, allocate the money you now have from the paid off debt to saving for retirement and continue to pay off any remaining debt. At this point in your life, you're much closer to retirement and need to begin to take advantage of employer matching and tax-deferred contributions.

Now, the key is to make sure you're not incurring any new debt and have a debt payoff plan. Otherwise, you won't change your situation. Ten years could go by and you'd still be in the same place financially.

Keep Up With Your Accounts

As you switch jobs, you may forget that you had a pension here or there. (I was guilty of this once.) It's important to know what you'll have coming in during your retirement years. Contact all previous and current employers about your retirement plan with them. Ask for an estimate of your payout at retirement. Be sure to read all the notices you get in the mail about your retirement plan. They often discuss changes or updates to your benefits. Also, contact the Social Security Administration periodically to see what amount you may receive from them.

Only Have an Account With Your Employer?

Please do not only have a retirement account with your employer. Invest in an IRA on your own. None of us could miss the countless news stories about employees who lost everything when their employer's stock hit rock bottom. Many of you probably knew someone personally that this happened to. It's important to use various retirement investing strategies. In the event one account doesn't do so well, you'll still have money elsewhere to soften the blow.

Types of Employer Plans

401(k): This is a very common retirement plan offered by employers. It's a replacement for older pension plans. When you enroll in a 401(k), you can contribute a percentage of your pre-tax earnings into the plan.

The managers of the plan then invest the money into mutual funds to grow it over time. When you reach retirement age, you pay taxes on the money as you withdraw it.

This leads to significant tax savings over your working life. There are also significant tax penalties for withdrawing money early, though in some cases you can get a loan from the money that's been placed in one.

Many companies will match what you put in if you've worked for them for a number of years. So if you contribute 10% of your pre-tax paycheck, they will put in that same dollar amount, giving you a significant boost to your capital. There are varieties of these plans, such as a 403(b), which is reserved for educators and nonprofits; and a 457, which is offered to government employees.

Roth 401(k): This is a new form of 401(k) that combines the advantages of a 401(k) with an IRA. (More on that in a bit.) With a Roth 401(k), your contribution is taken out of your paycheck *after* taxes, but then there are no further taxes on anything earned in the account. The money you withdraw from the account after you retire isn't taxed either.

Thrift Savings Plan (TSP): Thrift Savings Plans are essentially 401(k) plans for military and civilian government employees. Employees contribute pre-tax dollars from their paychecks and the government agency they work for matches up to a certain percent of their salary. Just as with a 401(k), employees pay taxes upon withdrawing their savings and are penalized if they do so before reaching age 59½. There is also a Roth version of the TSP that allows employees to make after-tax contributions.

457 and 403(b): These types of accounts are used by nonprofits, public schools, colleges, and state and local governments. They operate much like the 401(k) where employees contribute pre-tax earnings out of their paycheck and taxes are deferred until the money is withdrawn at retirement. Unfortunately, withdrawals during retirement are taxed as regular income on these accounts, but the thought is that, in retirement, you'll be in a lower income tax bracket than when you were working.

There are also differences between these accounts and a 401(k) as it relates to distributions. With the 457 plan, you can withdraw your money without penalties if you leave the job, whether or not you're 59½. With the 403b, there's a 10% penalty for any kind of early withdrawal.

Individual Retirement Plans

Traditional Individual Retirement Arrangement (IRA): If your employer doesn't offer any of the plans that were just mentioned, you can go to any bank or brokerage firm and open up an individual retirement arrangement. An IRA is a tax-deferred account. The income in one doesn't have to be reported to the IRS until you withdraw it. After withdrawal, the money is taxed. There's a limit to how much you can put into an IRA every year, but it's high enough that you can build a very nice nest egg. Once the money is in the account, you can invest it however you like into many different types of securities. And just like a 401(k), you can't withdraw the money from the account before retirement age without significant penalties.

Roth IRA: A Roth IRA takes after-tax dollars and puts them into an IRA account. Because you make contributions after taxes, you don't have to worry about paying more taxes on any money that's added to the account. It's very common to have both a 401(k) and a Roth IRA for a complete investment package. The 401(k) provides long-term benefits while the Roth IRA can be used for emergencies between now and retirement, and still provide a solid retirement nest egg. The contribution limit in a Roth is similar to that of a standard IRA.

SIMPLE IRA: This is a form of 401(k) for small businesses. A company can have no more than 100 employees in order to be eligible for this kind of plan. From an employee point of view, this type of account is very similar to a 401(k). If you're an employer, you'll pay less into the plan than you would a 401(k).

SIMPLIFIED EMPLOYEE PENSION PLAN (SEP IRA): If you're completely self-employed and have no one working for you, then the SEP IRA is the way to go. SEP IRAs are great if the income you're bringing in far exceeds the limit you can put into an IRA. There's no IRS filing requirement for this plans and the paperwork is minimal. However, determining how much you can contribute each year can be a little confusing. If you're going for the maximum contribution, it's around 25% of your net profit.

Whichever of these plans is right for you, it's better to get started earlier rather than later. The more you put in earlier, the larger your investment has a chance to grow over time. Just because your job doesn't offer a 401(k) doesn't mean you can't start saving for retirement now. Talk with your financial advisor for more information about these plans and what you can do to start making contributions right away. If you're nearing or at retirement age, AARP is one of the best sites to go to for information. Go to www.aarp.org. Also, be sure to check out www.myretirementblog.com/.

CHAPTER 10

Retirement Investing for Young Adults – Manyell Akinfe-Reed

#MoneyChat

Don't simply retire from something; have something to retire to.

HARRY EMERSON FOSDICK

THE ECONOMIC LANDSCAPE FOR YOUNG adults today is a lot different than it was for the generation before them. Not long ago, achieving the American Dream was a sure shot. You worked for 30 years; invested in a defined contribution plan, such as a 401(k) or 403(b); put money aside for a rainy day and retired with a hefty pension. Without a doubt you'd be able to buy a home and send your kids to school. Everything would inevitably work out if you just worked hard. Unfortunately, the terrain for Generations X and Y has been rockier. They've seen unemployment skyrocket, financial markets explode, education costs soar, a housing market crash and pensions vanish. While we'll never be able to control the market, young adults can stack the odds in their favor by avoiding common mistakes when preparing for their future.

Avoid Wasting Time

• •

Time is the most powerful asset young adults have when preparing for retirement, yet only 56% of workers ages 25–34, and 63% of workers ages 35–44, say they've begun saving[1]. For most of us, just thinking about saving enough is daunting. According to the retirement calculators I've used, I'll need $1.8 million to retire comfortably by age 67. Looking at all my current responsibilities and thinking of future ones, this number would drive me mad if I didn't understand that putting time on my side increases the number of years my money will grow and decreases the monthly amount I need to set aside.

Let's look at it in action. If you had a choice between receiving $100,000 toward your retirement today or a penny that doubled for 30 years, which would you choose? Most would choose the $100,000 and miss out on a whopping $10.7 million.

Grow, Penny, Grow

Years	Interest Earned	Your Balance
1	$0.01	$0.02
2	$0.02	$0.04
3	$0.04	$0.08
4	$0.08	$0.16
5	$0.16	$0.32
10	$5.12	$10.24
15	$163.84	$327.68
20	$5,242.88	$10,485.76
25	$167,772.16	$335,544.32
30	$5,368,708.80	$10,737,417.00

Although financial institutes don't offer an annual percentage rate of 100%, the above example illustrates the power of compound interest. Compound interest is the concept of earning interest on top

---

1   2013 Retirement Confidence Survey, Employee Benefit Research Institute and Mathew Greenwald & Associates

of interest. It's the reason a penny can grow to $10 million dollars without another cent being added to the account. Each year, the dollar amount of interest earned increases in response to a growing balance. Without compounding, the account would have only gained $0.01 a year and grown to a measly $0.30. You can apply this same concept to a more realistic example and get the same shocking results. A 25-year-old contributing $100 a month to a retirement account until age 67 and receiving an annual 6% in interest will amass $212,296! And 6% is a very conservative return. For a 25-year-old whose portfolio is properly allocated to include more exposure to stocks, we can expect to see an 8% return. Using the same monthly contribution and retirement age, the account would grow to $367,626.

Getting a head start saving will also lower your monthly retirement bill, making it easier to fit into your budget. Let's say the same 25-year-old above, earning the 8%, discovered they would need $800,000 to retire comfortably. To achieve this goal they would need to save $285[2] dollars a month. If this same person delays saving until age 35, they would need to save $588[3] per month. That additional $303 a month could be used to pay off debt, save for college or take a vacation. What the money is used for is insignificant compared to the high price that's paid for procrastinating.

---

2 Monthly amount assumes 15% marginal tax rate with no annual increase to savings.
3 Monthly amount assumes 15% marginal tax rate with no annual increase to savings.

Action Steps: Level Set!

1. **Don't freak out.**

    It's easy to get paralysis of analysis and dwell on how much you'll need. Accept that it's a big number and start working on a plan.

2. **Fast forward.**

    The amount you'll need in retirement will depend on several variables, such as the age you start saving, when you want to retire, your life expectancy, how much you plan to withdraw annually and much more. Before determining how much you need, you'll have to spend some time thinking about what you want your golden years to look like.

3. **Determine how much you'll need in retirement.**

    Less than half of all workers have tried to calculate how much they're going to need to save for retirement[4]. There's no way to develop an effective strategy if you don't know what you're aiming for. The Internet offers a wide selection of retirement calculators for free. When deciding which calculator to use, select the one that allows for the highest number of variables you could think of in the Fast Forward exercise above. The calculator should also give explanations for each field available so that you're clear on the assumptions used to calculate the recommended amount. I like the Ultimate Retirement Calculator on millionaire and financial coach Todd Tresidder's website. It's available for free.

---

4 2013 Retirement Confidence Survey, Employee Benefit Research Institute and Mathew Greenwald & Associates

Take the Money on the Table
. . . .

Young adults are leaving far too much money on the table. If your employer matches contributions made to their retirement plan, you should at least be making the minimum contribution to receive the match—PERIOD! The one caveat is that you pay very close attention to the fees you're being charged in your plan. If your plan is too expensive, it may be in your best interest to consider an alternate investment vehicle.

In 2012, the Department of Labor's Employee Benefits Security Administration released a rule that now requires employers to provide fee disclosures to participants in 401(k)-type plans. The information provided must include what was actually charged or deducted from your account, along with a description of what the charge was for. Previously, this information was not available and many employees had no idea how much it was costing them to participate in their employer retirement plan. According to a survey conducted by AARP, 71% of respondents didn't even know they were paying fees[5]. Having this information not only gives us the opportunity to decide if we're paying too much, it also enables us to consider these expenses in our retirement planning.

The fees and expenses in your plan will fall into two categories: administrative and investment. Administrative fees pay for your being a part of the plan and investment fees are associated with your individual investment choices.

Administrative charges cover the day-to-day operation of the plan, such as record keeping and customer service. This charge can be picked up by your company, covered by your investment fee or charged directly to the plan. When charged directly to the plan, the expense will get passed on to you as a flat fee or divided between all plan participants in proportion to their account balance. When passed

---

5 401(k) Participants' Awareness and Understanding of Fees, AARP Research & Strategic Analysis, 2011

on to plan participants, individuals with higher balances pay a higher percentage of the expense.

Investment fees, the larger of the two expenses, pay for the cost of managing the investments in the plan. These fees are deducted from your investment returns and depend on the type of investments you select, as well as the company providing the service. When reviewing your investment choices, you want to pick options with the lowest expenses. As a general rule of thumb, you should aim to pay no more than 1% in administrative fees and less than 1.5% for any given investment in your plan.

A half of a percentage may not seem like a lot of money, but over time it can significantly reduce your account balance as seen below.

You can't guarantee performance but you can guarantee that you won't pay high fees.

Action Steps: Do Your Research!

1. See how your plan stacks up.

Visit the Bright Scope website, (www.brightscope.com), to see how your plan compares to the plans of similar companies of the same size. The analysis will provide you with a good snapshot of your plan and expenses.

2. Check whether your company picks up the tab.

There are administrative expenses associated with running the plan that your employer is responsible for. In large companies, this expense is not passed on to the employees. However, in some smaller companies it is. Ask your plan sponsor if you are responsible for this expense.

3. Review your investment expenses.

   a. Secure a copy of your most recent investment statement. If you're not currently enrolled in your plan, you can either perform this review on all the funds available in your plan or preselect funds you are interested in.

   b. Look for the expense ratio for each fund you want to analyze. You can find this information on your 401(k) website or in the fund prospectus. Expense ratios are expressed as an annual percentage of your total investments.

   c. Calculate and find the total annual cost of each investment by multiplying the fund's expense ratio by your ending balance. For example, if you have $3,000 in an investment and its expense ratio is 0.20%, then you're paying $6 a year. You want to shoot for a total expense ratio between 1-1.5%.

4. **Make a decision.**

Once you've discovered your final cost and compared it to comparable plans, you can make an educated decision about whether to participate in your employer's plan.

The Four Stages of Retirement Planning

Allocate Appropriately

Proper asset allocation is essential to reaching your retirement goals. Although there is no one-size-fits-all formula, as a young investor, your time horizon should always be tightly knit to your risk tolerance. Your time horizon is the number of years you have to invest and your risk tolerance is your willingness and ability to handle fluctuations in the stock and bond markets. A basic investment strategy is to take more risk when you have a long time horizon, and less risk when you don't. With the number of years your money will need to last increasing with life expectancy, the age-old goal of $1M is likely not enough. By using the four stages of retirement planning outlined below as a guide, you can rest assured that you've done your part in setting your portfolio up for optimal growth.

Stage 1: Accumulation

The accumulation stage starts as soon as you have a job. If you're under 21, you probably won't be able to invest in your employer's plan. But any investor with earned income can open an Individual Retirement Account (IRA). In this first stage of your retirement planning, amassing wealth is your primary objective. Therefore, I recommend a portfolio of 85–100% stocks. By investing in stocks, you expose your portfolio to more risk in exchange for a higher return. This level of exposure will surely have its ups and downs, but understanding historical performance will help you stay the course.

The S&P 500 is the most commonly used benchmark for the U.S. stock market. Over the past 32 years, it has averaged a return of 11.2%. Calculated in this return are the major dips the stock market took that both Generation X and Y experienced, including its -37% return in 2008. The Barclays Capital Aggregated Bond Index, which is the benchmark for bonds, returned only 8.5% over the same period. That's a 2.7% difference! You'll need the high returns of the stock market to lay the foundation for your savings, and this is the only stage where you can take high risks because of the time you'll have to recover from losses.

Stage 2: Preservation

The preservation stage starts nine to 10 years before you retire. During this stage, your focus is on protecting your money. The old school of investing would suggest reducing your stock exposure to below 50%. I strongly suggest a 50/50 split between stocks and bonds. During this stage, I recommend hiring a fee-only advisor to go over your retirement goals and discuss with you whether you should scale back further from stocks. Your advisor will be able to give you a deeper understanding of the direction of the markets. Nearly one in four investors ages 56 to 65 had more than 90% percent of their account balances in stocks going into 2008, according to the Employee Benefit Research Institute. I don't know what age these individuals planned to retire, but I can guarantee you their timelines have been altered due to the effects the downturn had on their portfolio. No one can guarantee returns but a good financial advisor can make you aware of trends in the market that you should avoid or take advantage of.

Stage 3: Distribution

This is the stage in which you have retired and your objective is to ensure that your money is outpacing inflation. Let's assume an inflation rate between 2.5% to 3%. During this time, you should have 75%–85% of your money invested in bonds. Don't risk your savings, regardless of how well the market is performing, unless you are okay with the possibility of running out of money. There will be little to no time for recovering from a major downturn in the economy.

Stage 4: Transfer

The final stage, which is too often forgotten, is the transfer stage. Who do you want to reap the benefits of your hard work? Be sure that the beneficiaries on all your accounts are up to date. Retirement assets pass directly to beneficiaries without having to go through the long and costly process of probate court. Although your beneficiaries will avoid probate, they still may be responsible for federal and state income taxes on the money they receive. Inform your beneficiaries of this and provide them with a copy of any forms that name them as such. Make them aware that there may be tax liabilities associated with their payout so they're not caught by surprise.

Action Steps: What is Your Risk Tolerance?

1. **Assess your risk tolerance.**

   There are a slew of risk tolerance surveys on the Internet. A Google search returned 1,650M results, so you won't have trouble finding a few to take. Even if you think you know your risk tolerance and have been investing for some time, it's good to take part in this exercise. It may reveal information that was hidden before.

2. **Decide if you will follow.**

   The purpose of risk tolerance questionnaires is to give you direction. They're not intended to be a one-stop shop for asset allocation. You will ultimately tailor your final allocations based on things no questionnaire can address, such as your fear of losing money because your mom lost her savings when the dotcom bubble burst, or your love of bonds because you saw your grandma play it safe and win. In this step, you'll need to consider how much money you have to risk, what risk you're required to take to meet your goals and the effects different levels of risk have on your portfolio. If you're already saving for retirement, you can use portfolio analysis software on sites like PersonalCapital.com and Morningstar. com to see if your current asset allocation is where you want it. If it's not, you can adjust your percentages in each fund until they are aligned with where you want them going forward. Both sites provide commentary that can be used to guide your decisions. For new investors, making a decision will require a little more leg work. I suggest selecting a Target-Date Fund from either your employer's retirement plan or a company like Fidelity or Vanguard and inputting the fund's information into the sites I mentioned for portfolio analysis. Target-Date Funds are a mixture of different funds that are allocated based on the date you want to retire. As you get closer to retirement, your stock exposure decreases. Using Target-Date Funds as a guide will help you determine how similar or different you need your asset allocation to be.

3. **Take action.**

After you've spent time exploring risk and determining the approach you want to take, it's time to take action. If you're still unsure, ask for help. Every financial company that offers products has customer service representatives that can answer questions about the investments they provide. They won't be able to give you financial advice but they can give you general information on the investment and its performance. Some employers provide access to financial advisors free of charge. Check with your employer to see if this is available to you.

Final Thoughts

Putting time on your side, taking advantage of your employers match and having the proper asset allocation is just the beginning of your investing journey. Throughout your trip you will need to remain positive, perform regular checkups and maintain a long term perspective. For the majority of us saving for retirement is the largest financial goal we will have to accomplish. You can borrow money for college or to buy a house but here are no loans for retirement. Social security will offer some assistance but proper planning will always be the cornerstone of a long term investment strategy. With the cost of living increases, staggering health care cost and a troubled social security system we must be proactive in planning our financial future to accumulate an adequate retirement fund.

1. **Maintain a positive attitude.**
   Don't look at saving as a burden. Focus on how you'll feel once you've reached your goal and take pride in knowing you're taking steps to plan your tomorrow today.

2. **Perform checkups.**
   Examine your progress at least twice a year. Make sure you're on track to retire at your desired age. Confirm that your money will last throughout retirement and that you'll be able to afford the lifestyle you want during retirement. Here is where the Ultimate Retirement Calculator I mentioned previously can help.

3. **Keep a long-term perspective.**
   Sometimes you'll look at your balance and feel like you'll never reach your goal. You'll come up with a million and one reasons to withdraw your money. Don't do it! Remember—you can only replace lost time with more money, and who's signing up for that?

FINANCIAL EXPERT MANYELL AKINFE-REED IS the founder of The Money Movement, a social campaign designed to use pop culture to promote financial responsibility. She is a Reuters, CNBC and Black Enterprise Business Report contributor and an active volunteer for several community programs increasing the financial literacy of New Yorkers.

Connect with Manyell!
Visit: www.moneymovement.org
Twitter: @ManyellAkinfe

CHAPTER 11
Saving for College

"Education is our passport to the future, for tomorrow belongs to the people who prepare for it today."

MALCOLM X

What College Will Likely Cost in Five, 10, 20 Years

IN ITS MOST RECENT *Trends in College Pricing* study, the College Board reported that tuition increased by 6% from 2011 to 2012—much more than the rate of inflation, which was only 1.3%. While that's definitely a big jump, it's not surprising. Historically, college tuition prices double every 10 to 12 years and, from the looks of things, that's not about to change. The cost of higher education is going to get, well, *higher*! In fact, many experts estimate that the average cost of a four-year education will be $250,000 by the year 2020.

On average, you can expect college expenses to increase between 5% and 7% each year. Knowing that, you can estimate what college will likely cost when your child graduates from high school, whether that's in five years or 17 years. There's a quick and easy calculator on finaid.org that you can use to determine how much money you'll need to save for college. When you calculate, be sure to include all costs; not only tuition but room and board, books and other expenses. Then start saving as soon as you can, the earlier the better. A 529 Savings Plan and a Coverdell ESA are two tax-advantaged investment accounts we'll talk about in this book that you'll want to look into.

Why Does It Cost So Much?

Colleges receive money from a variety of sources:

- Tuition and fees

- Federal, state and local (city) funds

- Endowment income (money or property donated to an institution)

Schools need this money to cover their expenses, which include hiring quality professors, making improvements to the facility and so on. Over time, buildings age, technology changes and expenses rise. This means income sources must keep pace. How schools do this appears to differ between public and private institutions, however. According to the Delta Cost Project, both types of colleges rely on tuition and fees but "increases in tuition and fees were the single largest source of revenue for private institutions, while state and local appropriations remain the largest revenue category for public institutions." (Source: The Growing Imbalance, http://www.deltacostproject.org) This is a good reason to take a long, hard look at the cost differences between a public and private education.

Make a Plan. And Stick to It.

Whether your children are toddlers or teenagers, it's never too late or too early to start saving for college. Of course, the amount you can save will be based on your budget and household expenses. But it's important to set a goal, even if you'll have to begin later. Don't allow the costs of college to overwhelm you. Do what you can. Create a strategy for where you are now, and stick to it.

Do the math

1. How long do you have before your child/children graduate high school?

2. How much can you afford to set aside each month?

Let's say the average cost of college, whether private or public, is $25,000 per year. Remember that this amount fluctuates depending on the school. It also doesn't take into consideration inflation or annual tuition increases, but it's a good starting point. So let's crunch the numbers.

Average annual cost of college:
$25,000 x 4 years = $100,000
Number of years until your child graduates = 7
$100,000/7 years = $14,285 per year
$14,285/12 mos. = $1,190 = the amount you would need to save each month for the next seven years

Whoa! That's a lot of money, right? Okay, don't panic.

Of course, the younger your children are, the more time you have to save. So if you have a newborn to elementary student and have disposable income, you're in great shape. But let's suppose you can't put away the amount suggested in our example above. The average family can't put $1,200 toward college savings each month. In fact, many families already have children in high school already and haven't been able to save much at all. Don't get discouraged. Look at your personal finances and decide on a reasonable amount you can invest each month. Now develop a plan each year to increase that amount.

Based on our example, the college-bound child is in the sixth grade (because the parent(s) have seven years to save). Here's the plan the child's parent(s) developed to set aside college funds. (This is a basic college savings plan. It doesn't take into consideration the interest that will accrue and increase the funds available.)

# of Years	Monthly Savings	Annual Savings	Total
Year 1	150	1,800	1,800
Year 2	200	2,400	4,200
Year 3	250	3,000	7,200
Year 4	300	3,600	10,800
Year 5	300	3,600	14,400
Year 6	350	4,200	18,600
Year 7	350	4,200	22,800

As you can see, this child's parent(s) will end up with $22,800 when the child is graduating high school! Now, that may not cover all four years, but it will definitely cover one year. And depending on the school, it may even cover two years.

Another thing to consider is that you can continue to sock away money while your child is in college for the next three years. Whether you're able to save more or less each year, it's important to develop a plan for the time you have. Being able to get an idea of how the savings will add up over the years allows parents to research additional resources—such as scholarships, dual enrollment, work study, etc.—to make up the difference.

Do Your Homework

Begin researching schools, criteria for qualifying for scholarships and other potential tuition-reducing programs. For example, students who serve as resident assistants in their dorms during their junior and senior years won't have to pay for room and board those two years.

In planning for your children's college education, keep one thing in mind: Generally, no one pays the sticker price, that is, the actual, quoted cost of attending a particular school before grants and other financial aid is applied. Regardless of your income, you probably won't either. If you find that the costs are more than you want to pay, community college is an excellent option for your child's first two years of college.

Action Steps: Offset the Rising Cost of College!

Here are a few things you can begin doing now to offset the rising cost of college:

1. Use this calculator to determine what college will cost by the time your children are ready to attend.

2. Look at your household budget and determine how much you can begin to save for each of your children. Contact your financial advisor to determine what type of college savings investment plan is best for you.

3. Prepare your children academically—via tutoring, enrichment programs, etc.—so they'll do well in class and on college entrance exams. This will make them attractive candidates for scholarships and grants when they apply to colleges.

Deciding Where to Put It

You've decided to invest for your children's education—kudos to you! Now where to save may be a slightly tougher decision. We're here to help! Below are four college savings investing options for you to evaluate. Consider which one—or which combination—is best for your family.

529 College Savings Plans

529 College Savings Plans are a very attractive solution for saving for college. They were created in 1996 in Section 529 of the IRS code—hence its name. They are essentially mutual funds for college savings, so they contain a mix of investments in stocks, bonds, real estate and money market funds. Over the life of the account, contribution limits range from $100,000–$300,000, based on the rules of your state, and your money grows tax-free. And you're not limited to investing in a 529 Plan in the state you live in. If another state offers the best plan for your goals, you can invest there. Another good thing about 529 Plans are their low investment minimums. In most cases, you can open an account with as little as $25. There's also no age limit on beneficiaries or time limit on distributions.

Eligibility: There are no limitations on eligibility for a 529 Plan. Anyone can open an account.

Taxes: You won't pay any federal taxes if the money is used for qualified school expenses: tuition, books, fees, room and board. Normally, you wouldn't pay any state taxes either, but each state sets its own rules. You can't deduct 529 Plan contributions on your federal income taxes, but some states allow a tax deduction.

While you may be able to contribute large amounts in one year—be careful. You could incur a gift tax if you go over the maximum gift allowance of 13,000 per year. Stay below this annual maximum to make sure you avoid this tax.

Returns: A Word to the Wise

Pay attention to the investments in the 529 Plan you choose. There are various options based on the age of your student and your risk tolerance. Remember to research the investments contained in the plans. Do they have solid returns of 8%–10% or more over a 10-year period? If not, you may want to choose another state's plan. Financial advisors and their clients are noticing that some 529 Plans aren't performing as well as expected. They're getting the same return you would get from simply having your money in a savings account! Ouch!

Coverdell Education Savings Accounts (ESAs)

Coverdell ESAs, also known as Education IRAs, are another option for saving for college that also invests in stocks, CDs, mutual funds, bonds and money market funds. You can only contribute $2,000 per year, but that's a great starting point for many families until they are able to contribute more. Since you contribute after-tax earnings, the money is withdrawn tax-free when your child is ready for college. The beneficiary must be under 18 when the account is opened and the money has to be used by the child's thirtieth birthday.

There are limitations on who can contribute to a Coverdell ESA:

- If you're single, your annual income must be under $95,000.

- If you're married, your annual income must be under $190,000.

Other State-Sponsored Savings Plans

Many states offer savings plans that help you save for your child's college now. Basically, these programs allow you to pre-pay a part of your child's tuition before he or she is ready to go to college. This gives the child a huge head start and makes it much easier to budget out the costs of college over time. A prime example of a state-sponsored savings plan is the Michigan Education Trust (https://www.michigan.gov/setwithmet). Others can be found via the College Savings Plans Network website (http://www.collegesavings.org/index.aspx).

One caveat is that the money in many state-sponsored savings programs must be used for public, in-state schools. Some programs may offer a refund that allows you to apply the money to other schools, but it may not be the same amount as if your child stayed in state. Further, the money saved in these programs can only go toward tuition. It doesn't cover other college-related expenses, such as room and board, and books. You can, however, transfer the funds to siblings or first cousins if, for some reason, the original recipient chooses not attend college.

Mutual Funds

Mutual funds are not the best types of investment for your child's education because you'll be taxed on the capital gains you earn each year. It can work if you have a fund that's outperforming each year, thus offsetting the taxes you'd have to pay. But I'm not so sure it's worth the hassle when you have other college savings options. Also, the contributions you make to a mutual fund aren't tax deductible. If anything, mutual funds as a college savings vehicle should be a last resort.

What about using a 401(k) or other retirement accounts?

Your children will have many options for paying for college when the time comes. You, on the other hand, will not when it comes to your retirement. And nine times out of 10, your children will not be in a position to help you. Guard your retirement savings like a hawk and keep them intact. Definitely do not raid it to pay for college expenses.

The key is to definitely have a college savings strategy. Don't feel like a bad parent if you can't pay 100% of your child's tuition, especially if you have more than one child. Again, there are several options for paying for college. You don't have to deplete your personal or retirement savings.